HOPE BEYOND

To Jerome + Lana, dear friends

Thank you for the fellowship we've had together and for being participants in the home study group at Jimmie's + Gary's house. He, God, manifested Himself, in ways of His love, to all of us. Until I began writing this testimony, I didn't know how timely and strategic that home group was for my spiritual growth + journey.

Jerome – God wanted me to remind you that He loves you as one of His favorite sons. God, the Father, choose's the ordinary to do extraordinary things.

Lana – "Continue to grow in intimacy with Him for it will bring depth and understanding into the ways of our Lord. He's well pleased with your progress and will honor your every effort."

Ferel?

To Jerome & Lana, dear friends, a brother & sister in Christ—

A   S P I R I T U A L   M E M O I R

May the Holy Spirit anoint these words bringing new revelation and understanding for your spiritual journey as you read,

HOPE BEYOND

How God Orchestrates Time, People, and Events to Bring About His Purpose for Your Life and His Kingdom

Numbers 6:24-25

Ferel

FEREL LITTLE

1-29-2022

Hope Beyond

© 2021 Ferel Little.

ISBN (Print): 979-8-9854811-0-5

ISBN (Kindle): 979-8-9854811-1-2

Library of Congress Control Number: 2021925595

Printed in the United States of America

Published by Ferel LIttle | Bryan, Texas

Prepared for Publication: www.wendykwalters.com

To contact the author: www.f e r e l l i t t l e .com

Scripture translations used:

Unless otherwise noted, scripture quotations are taken from the HOLY BIBLE, NEW INTERNATIONAL VERSION®. Copyright © 1973, 1978, 1984 by International Bible Society. Used by permission of Zondervan Publishing House. All rights reserved.

Scripture quotations marked AMP are from the Amplified® Bible. Copyright © 1954, 1958, 1962, 1964, 1965, 1987, 2015 by The Lockman Foundation. La Habra, CA. Used by permission.

Scripture quotations marked ESV are from The Holy Bible, English Standard Version®. ESV® Text Edition: 2016. Copyright © 2001 by Crossway, a publishing ministry of Good News Publishers.

Scripture quotations marked KJV are from the King James Version of the Bible®. Copyright © 1982 by Broadman & Holman Publishers, Nashville, TN. Used by permission. All rights reserved.

Scripture quotations marked MSG are from The Message®. Copyright © 1993, 1994, 1995, 1996, 2000, 2001, 2002. Used by permission of NavPress Publishing Group. Colorado Springs, CO. All rights reserved.

Scripture quotations marked NKJV are from the New King James Version of the Bible. Copyright © 1982 by Thomas Nelson, Inc. Used by permission. All rights reserved.

Scripture quotations marked TPT are from The Passion Translation®. Copyright © 2017, 2018, 2020 by Passion & Fire Ministries, Inc. Used by permission. All rights reserved. ThePassionTranslation.com.

DEDICATION

To God the Father, Jesus the Son, and the Holy Spirit who gave
the words to write and make this journey possible.

To two wonderful companions—in memory
of Nita who co-labored in ministry,
and in honor of Sue who co-labored in prayer as well as
supporting and encouraging this book.

To every faithful and obedient follower of our Lord
who assisted in the many divine appointments
shared in this spiritual memoir.

ACKNOWLEDGMENT

Thank you, Wendy Walters, for the wonderful job
editing and helping to publish this book.

DISCLAIMER

PRAISE FOR HOPE BEYOND

I met Ferel in the early 1980s. I was a Methodist pastor, and Ferel was in the oil and gas business. We were involved with a group of believers pursuing God and His Kingdom in East Texas, and I learned that Ferel had once been an ordained pastor. As our friendship grew, I invited him to preach in the church I served. He shared some of his experiences of being a part of a mission trip to South America.

I moved to a church in South East Texas and soon found out that Ferel had reentered the ministry and was serving a church only 18 miles away. We renewed our friendship and enjoyed our fellowship and ministry, and later we were both appointed to churches in N.E. Texas. Our friendship grew, and even in retirement, we have stayed in contact.

I have the highest respect for Ferel. He is a man of integrity, a faithful pastor and preacher, serving God and the Kingdom everywhere he goes. I commend to you his life, ministry, and witness. It is all for the glory of God and for extending the Kingdom.

BLUFORD WEIKEL
Retired Pastor

I have had the privilege and blessing to share life with Ferel for nearly 20 years, and throughout this time, he has been my pastor, spiritual mentor, and most of all, my friend. Our lives have been intertwined over the years by efforts, but even more so through God's divine hand that seems to cause the trajectory of our lives suddenly to come back together for a season. God used Ferel to speak a supernatural promise or truth over my life, and at times over the life of my husband as well as my children and generations to follow. The timing of Ferel's words always proves to be God's perfect timing, and I am so thankful for Ferel's persistence in pressing into the Heart of the Father for His children and the boldness to speak what he hears.

MRS. BECKY HAND
Friend

Though I have not known Ferel long, I have gotten to experience him through our journey of preparing this manuscript for publishing. Hope Beyond is a powerful story of God's promise, purpose, and provision. Ferel shares his testimony of God's supernatural intervention in his life in a way that will build your faith and hopefully make you hungry to experience more of the supernatural in your life as well.

WENDY K. WALTERS
Author, Editor, Ghostwriter

Contents

"WE HAVE THIS HOPE
AS AN ANCHOR FOR THE SOUL,
FIRM AND SECURE.
IT ENTERS THE INNER SANCTUARY
BEHIND THE CURTAIN,
WHERE JESUS,
WHO WENT BEFORE US,
HAS ENTERED ON OUR BEHALF."

HEBREWS 6:19-20A

INTRODUCTION

"THERE IS A TIME FOR EVERYTHING,
AND A SEASON FOR EVERY ACTIVITY UNDER HEAVEN:
A TIME TO BE BORN AND A TIME TO DIE ..."

ECCLESIASTES 3:1–2A

Most agree we have only one life to live. How we choose to live that life is up to each of us. It's a choice that every person makes throughout their life. I believe we only have two options: choose to live life with God through Jesus Christ, or choose to live life by other secular influences or religions that the world offers. From the time we take our first breath until the time we take our last, life is a journey based upon the daily choices that we make. Most choices provide either positive results or negative consequences; very few are neutral. Sometimes our lives may take an unexpected turn of events based upon circumstances that we have no control over. This may be caused by many things, such as an unexpected sickness, loss of employment, an untimely death of a loved one, or a tragic accident. Sometimes our lives are affected by external events such as social disruption, global upheaval, or the recent pandemic of Covid–19, which began in 2019.

Sometimes, however, our lives are impacted so suddenly and dramatically by a person or an event that it stops us in our tracks resulting in a new direction or understanding. Have you ever had anything like that happen to you? It's similar to a songwriter who suddenly recalled a memory that turned into the next hit song. It's like a chance meeting with an old friend who gave you a tip about a new job opening that later led to your hiring and a successful career. It's like hearing a song, reading a poem, walking on a nature trail, or perhaps gazing upon a classic piece of art when something happened within you that transformed and turned your life instantly one hundred and eighty degrees. This may have resulted in a new direction for your life totally different from how you had been living, or a recommitment to a purpose that you had been apathetic about in your present journey, or even exploring new areas of service outside of self. How do you view such happenings? I've heard people say that it was just plain luck or coincidence. I have heard others remark that it was destiny or perhaps an answer to a prayer.

People who know me will probably say, and I will agree, that I am an ordinary person. Like so many, I have some talents and abilities; but I would desire many more. I was blessed with parents who gave me opportunities they did not have, and I have tried to do the same for my children. My life's journey has been filled with success and failure, with joy and sadness, death and life. I have loved, been loved, and continue to love. Even though my desire was to love perfectly, my actions and words sometimes betrayed me. A wise man once said, *"I do not understand what I do. For what I want to do I do not do, but what I hate I do"* (Romans 7:15). To my many acquaintances, friends, and loved ones who I have disappointed, failed, or hurt, I can only confess: "Forgive me!"

My desire in writing this book is to entice the "believer" who has a "religion of the mind" to discover a "Jesus of the heart" that leads to greater intimacy and spiritual maturity with Him. My challenge to "the unbeliever" is to travel these uncharted waters with an open mind, heart, and spirit and discover that these events are not mere coincidences that happened. For me, such events are divine appointments. Divine appointments shatter the mindsets of many believers and unbelievers alike, astounding the wise. Every event was the direct result of a God who orchestrates time, people, and events to bring about His purpose for their lives and His kingdom on earth as it is in heaven. Divine appointments manifest God's unfailing love for those involved in real-time events to build faith and encourage the believer and unbeliever alike.

Divine appointments, I believe, help shift the mindsets of the hardest of hearts who have been deceived. What seems so insignificant to others at that moment may be the most important time or word received for the other. God places you there in that divine moment to bring forth His message of grace, deliverance, restoration, and reconciliation. Personal faith is either born, deepened, or rejected whenever a person experiences the unexplainable; because we cannot deny what we have seen and heard. The same is true whenever when we accept the testimony of others, as I hope that you accept this writing as my testimony to you. We don't have to understand it—only to rejoice and to be glad in that moment! "*(Then) he (the crippled beggar) jumped to his feet and began to walk. Then he went with them into the temple courts, walking and jumping, and praising God*" *(Acts 3:8)*.

My heartfelt desire is for every person to discover that God's love for me is no more special than His love is for them. Together, we will *"... give thanks to the Lord for his unfailing love and his wonderful deeds for men" (Psalm 107:31).*

I invite you to come on this journey with me. Together, we will discover a God who delights in doing extraordinary things through ordinary people. Together, we will discover a God who orchestrates time, people, and events so that every person can live life to the fullest and partner with Him in bringing about His will on earth. *"For we are God's workmanship, created in Christ Jesus to do good works, which God prepared in advance for us to do" (Ephesians 2:10).*

Join me on this journey. Together, we will connect with a heavenly Father who will manifest His love to us as we discover **Hope Beyond.**

CHAPTER 1

LADY IN THE STREET

It was approaching 3:00 pm on a clear, crisp February Friday in 1981. I stepped out the front door of my office, looking forward to meeting my golf buddies. All afternoon, the hands on the clock had seemed to be standing still as I awaited the hour to approach. Finally, the time arrived, and I eagerly locked the door and left the office.

As I was crossing the street to meet my friends, I heard a voice call out my name, "Ferel, I want to talk to you."

Glancing to my right, a lady was walking towards me. I recognized her as a musician from church and knew that she worked in the building next door; otherwise, I had no social contact with her. I smiled politely and said, "Hi, Anna! I'm on my way to an appointment, but I will be glad to visit with you tomorrow."

Anna continued walking towards me, becoming more insistent, and said, "I really need to talk to you right now."

As I reached her side of the street, I turned and waited for her to walk up to me out of courtesy. She had a friendly disposition and smiled as she approached. As she drew near, she asked me a question that I had never been asked before by anyone, much less by an almost stranger, "Ferel, do you believe in prayer?"

Instantly, my mind went back several years to a seminary professor who told me that prayer was a figment of my imagination. I meekly answered, "Yes, I believe in prayer." As I said those words, I knew that I probably didn't believe in prayer like Anna did.

She replied, "Ferel, do you know what intercessory prayer is?"

My mind spun like a whirlwind. *What is going on?* I thought. I had pretty well kept my identity as a pastor who had left the pulpit a secret. No one knew that I'd gone to seminary. But I replied, "Yes, isn't intercessory prayer similar to standing in the gap and praying for someone?"

Anna nodded and replied, "That's good enough for you, now." She touched my arm lightly and said, "Earlier this week, I was praying in my favorite spot when suddenly your face appeared before me. It was as if you were standing there in the room, Ferel." I stepped back from her and took a deep breath. She leaned forward in earnest to continue her message.

I don't remember the exact details of what Anna said, but this woman earnestly believed that the Spirit of the Lord had given her a message to give me. Everything she said in the next few minutes related to specific events in my life—from the age of 16 all the way to that very moment. Her words connected joy and pain, hope and disappointment, success and failure all at the same time. Her gaze was unwavering, and she spoke with such conviction—her words penetrated deep within me! Thirty minutes later, I was weeping at the edge of the road. This lady had indeed heard from the Lord! She told me specific events, thoughts, and emotions that resonated within my spirit that she shouldn't know. When she finished, instant fear and reverence of the Lord overwhelmed me![1] I instantly believed and was convinced that if I didn't turn my life 180°, a lightning bolt from a cloudless sky would zap and leave me as a greasy spot in the dirt. As Anna finished her message, she grabbed me by the arm while looking straight into my eyes and said with firmness, "Tomorrow, I will pick you and your wife up for supper around 4:30 pm. We're driving to Lufkin, Texas, to hear a testimony from an oilman who says that God tells him where to drill to find oil. He gives 50% of his profit to wherever he believes that God tells him to give the money in support of various ministries."

Needless to say, my golf buddies hadn't waited for me. They went on without me that afternoon. I wasn't in any shape to join them anyway. This unforeseen meeting—this "divine appointment"—had shaken me to my inner core. I was weak in the knees and trembling as I walked back across the street to get into my pickup. Nothing like this had ever happened to me.

I was in a daze and decided to drive out to my small farm to think about this encounter. Sitting in my pickup underneath my favorite oak tree overlooking a pond, I was soon joined by my small herd of cows who thought I was there to feed them. After waiting patiently for me and then mooing their displeasure, they began to disperse slowly. I was in no mood to feed them at this time.

Anna meeting me in the street was a strange experience and encounter, to say the least, having been raised in a non-Pentecostal atmosphere. My mind began to wonder about events that her words connected with. My thoughts drifted back to an earlier time when I was six years old. It seemed like only yesterday. My parents and I had spent Christmas, 1946, with my grandmother in Clyde, Texas. It was a fun time because my favorite uncle, aunt, and cousins were also there. Returning home, I remember riding in a 1940 four-door Chrysler where the back doors opened from the front to the rear. Traveling with my parents from Snyder, Texas, heading home towards Carlsbad, New Mexico at 60 miles per hour, Sandy, my cocker spaniel whose hair was the color of white sand, and I were in the backseat. It was cold, and I wore a heavy coat with an attached hood. I had just shared some of my Christmas treat of chocolate-covered cherries with my parents when I decided to eat one more myself. As I raised it to my lips, Sandy suddenly lunged at me, deciding that he, not me, needed that chocolate-covered cherry. Instinctively, I moved backward because I didn't want him to eat my candy. The next thing I remember was rolling down the highway and coming to a stop. Jumping up, I began to run after the disappearing car. I was hollering, "Daddy! Mom! Wait for me!"

I try to imagine, today, what my parents felt like when they heard rushing wind suddenly enter the car along with a slamming door. Looking back over their shoulders, they saw a shut rear door with my heavy coat and hood hanging perfectly on it, but without me. Terrified, my dad braked the car harshly. Sandy was crouched down behind the other seat, scared. I'm sure my parents were relieved to see me running towards the car, but what they saw next would horrify them. I had blood all over my hands, face, and head as my mother held me in the front seat. My dad turned the car around so violently that it almost turned over as it headed back to the hospital in Snyder, Texas. My mom would later tell me after my dad had passed away that as he turned the car around, he was screaming at the top of his lungs, "Let him live, Lord! Let him live! I'll dedicate his life to you, Lord, just let him live!" I can still hear myself screaming as the doctor and nurses who attended to me poured iodine upon my head as they picked gravel from my scalp. Later, as I looked at my bandaged self in a mirror, my parents would tell me that I had 35 to 40 stitches in my forehead and one stitch on the tip of my nose. It was like I had made a 3-point landing.

Admitting me to the hospital, my parents kept me awake all night long. The doctors were afraid that I would have a concussion or brain swelling. The next morning, however, the doctor reported that he had seen a miracle because my x-rays and tests revealed no broken bones, no concussion, and no brain swelling. He further remarked, "Your son will heal from the bruises. Your doctor at home can monitor for infection and remove his stitches when needed; therefore, we will dismiss him today." The many stitches would leave three separate scars on my forehead. The middle scar would heal in the shape of a star.

Until that moment, while sitting at the farm thinking about the events of the day, I had never thought about falling out of a car going 60 miles an hour without encountering broken bones or a concussion as a miracle or supernatural event, even after what my mom had told me earlier, until now.

I jerked suddenly as my favorite cow, Old Gray, nudged my elbow at the pickup's open window. She was looking for her familiar treat. Luckily, I spotted two cattle cubes on the floorboard and gave them to her. She munched on them as she walked away.

My mind then drifted to when I was 16. I was attending a spring weekend at a nearby encampment. My local pastor had invited a friend of mine and me to attend this youth conference committed to recruiting young people into various forms of ministry. Following the last afternoon session, before the closing service that night, we walked to the river and sat down on the hillside overlooking the water. We agreed to separate so we could meditate privately about what we had heard. I enjoyed hearing the constant flow of the river and hearing sounds of nature. After thirty minutes or so, a light sprinkle of rain began to fall. Looking towards my friend further down on the river, I discovered that he had already gone back to the main camp. I arose to go back to shelter also. For some reason, however, I sat back down, thinking to myself that I would wait a few moments longer. *A little rain won't hurt me,* I thought. It seemed only a minute that I began to hear one bird calling in the distance on the other side of the river. The bird's call grew louder and louder. The crescendo was similar to an approaching train. Suddenly, I could hear no sounds at all. It was total serenity and peace. The words escaped from my mouth, "Yes Lord, here I am, send me."

As I opened the pickup door to get out and move about, I realized that sunset would arrive within the hour. It was time to go and leave some bales of hay for the livestock since they had gathered at the barn. Shutting the gate behind me, the drive back home began.

As I drove, immediately, my thoughts turned to the early years of ministry. Graduating high school at 17, I began serving rural student appointments throughout my college and seminary years, graduating seven years later. Getting married the summer before my senior year in college added joy to my life because my wife was loving, cheerful, and laughing all the time. I must confess that maintaining such a schedule kept me on the road constantly. I didn't have any quiet time to develop faith. Yes, I was in ministry; but I didn't have a deep, abiding faith that was needed to sustain me. My faith was more intellectual instead of heartfelt. From the professor who told me that prayer was a figment of my imagination to the liberal and modern theology being taught at the seminary, I felt that I had no faith. Congregations would be destroyed if believers heard what I had been taught. I had tried to preach faith until I developed it, but it didn't work. Ironically, success followed me in the churches I had served. Memberships grew, and budgets were met.

Sadly, there was a war going on in my soul. A desire to make money and fulfill the basic needs and desires of my wife and newborn son entered my thinking often. To put it simply, I was tired of feeling like a "charity case." Together with my lack of faith, I decided to act upon my feelings.

Hearing a seventy-year-old grandpa singing in the choir one Sunday, I couldn't help but smile. I loved this elderly man who sang with gusto and a loud voice even though he sounded like an off-key bullfrog on the riverbank. His eyes sparkled as he sang. They revealed his deep abiding faith to me that I knew he had and that I needed. This pastor suddenly realized that he had no business destroying his faith or the faith of any believer. I promised God that morning that I would return someday to the pulpit when I discovered my faith. That promise would lead to this book, *Hope Beyond*. Two weeks later, I resigned from the pulpit. Thirty days later, my wife and I relocated, where I began employment with an oil company in marketing.

The work was challenging yet rewarding. I was fortunate to receive three promotions along the way; however, my educational background kept me from advancing further. I received a lateral move to East Texas, thereby confirming that the upward progress stopped. I was devastated because success had been a driving force during this season of my life. Life was good and enjoyable at this time, but then I was faced with a fateful decision. The company told me that I had to move to a large urban area and become a retail salesman once again. That job was very stressful besides living in a major metropolitan area. I pleaded for them to leave me where I was in this small East Texas town. It was a great place to raise your family and to be a part of the community. They left me no choice but to move. I looked around to see what else I could do locally, but no employment opportunity existed to pay me the salary I had already attained. I was so determined not to go back to a major city that I resigned my position and took over a wholesale agency with the same company in a small East Texas town that cut my income in half.

My dad thought I had lost my mind once again. Not only had I left the pulpit, but I was also leaving a good income with benefits. Life was hard that first couple of years. I did most of the full-time deliveries with the help of a part-time driver, and my wife ran the office. My wife and I began to grow very tired and were soon exhausted. All work and no play left no time to be with the children and be a family together. One night after everyone had gone to bed, I laid down on the floor and began to cry like a baby. I said out loud, "Lord, I can't take it anymore. I need help." Immediately a feeling of deep peace fell upon me. My weeping stopped. I just knew that everything would be all right. About two weeks later, job seekers began to come by. I was able to hire two gentlemen who helped immensely. Many years later, my mom would tell me how dad was praying daily that I could not rest until I found my way back into the Lord and in His service. It's amazing what God will do.

Twilight was giving way to dark as I drove into the garage. *Wow! Could all of these events be connected?* I didn't realize at this moment just how dramatic and life-changing this event in the street would be. I entered the house where my lovely wife met me with her hands on her hips, saying, "Where have you been?"

I replied, "You won't believe all that has happened to me today!"

ENDNOTE

1. *"The fear of the Lord is the beginning of wisdom, and knowledge of the Holy One is understanding."* Proverbs 9:10.

CHAPTER 2

THE JOURNEY BEGINS

Throughout the weekend, I kept reliving the strange encounter with Anna. My mind was a whirlwind as I recounted what she said and tried to see the connection of past events to the current situation. The thought that God would send a lady into the street to give me a message just blew my mind. I had no concept of a God who acted this way. I had read about this type of event in the Bible, but my understanding was that miracles, signs, and wonders happened only in the first century. The one thing I knew was simply this; it happened. It couldn't be denied. This event would gradually transform my life, bring me back into an awareness of God's presence, and reawaken my shepherd's heart.

Anna invited me to attend her weekly Bible study, led by Spirit-filled people, from a church in another town. I had witnessed a sampling of "Spirit-filled people" at a Full Gospel Business Men's Fellowship dinner where we listened to the oil man who drilled wells where God told him to go. I did not know, however, what Spirit-filled meant as defined by these people. My encounter with that group had turned what little faith and spiritual understanding I possessed upside down. The words spoken to me were true and convincing, resulting in an instant reverential fear of God and doing whatever was necessary to transform my life 180° degrees for God. These reasons and my spiritual curiosity to know more overcame my timidity of the spiritual unknown. Nothing else mattered! I accepted her invitation.

I remember vividly that first meeting. These Christians were unlike any I had ever been around. They didn't worship like mainline denomination believers. They sang lustily with arms outstretched, clapping their hands and stomping their feet. I know that I stood out because I did none of these things, but they didn't seem to mind. It was certainly different than coming from a church background where you could usually hear a pin drop. All this seemed awkward to me. An awareness crept over me that day, however, that these believers had something that I didn't have, and I wanted it.

I couldn't define or rationalize what was happening. It was as if God was beginning to remove everything that I thought I knew about Him, which was very little. He began to teach me like a newborn babe with milk. I was witnessing formality and structure being replaced with informality and freedom of expression. This small band of believers had a sincere sense of love that I had not seen or felt before. The women especially reflected a sense of joy that consumed them. It took me several meetings before I became comfortable receiving or giving hugs from the men and women. It was difficult during that season in my life to show affection, to let go, and to worship in such freedom. But my hunger and desire for the spiritual increased. I would travel anywhere and read everything that would expand my spiritual understanding and horizon.

My desire to be filled with the Holy Spirit with the evidence of a prayer language became an obsession with me. People would pray for me at every meeting I attended to receive this gift, but to no avail. It was frustrating because I felt that some people would look at me as if something was wrong. *"We just don't understand why he's not getting this gift?"* Without knowing it, I was coming under a spirit of guilt and condemnation. I didn't like this feeling. After returning home from a meeting one night, Nita turned to me and said, "Why don't you get off into a corner by yourself? I'm tired of seeing you walk the aisle and being prayed for at every meeting. You're embarrassing me. I don't know where this is going, but I have no intentions of becoming a pastor's wife again. I like the life that we are living now. If God wants you to have whatever it is you're seeking, then go to your closet. He can give it to you there—or go out to the farm in solitude, but *stop* making a fool out of yourself and me—or I won't be going with you anymore to these meetings!" Her outburst shocked and stunned me. She went on to bed. I stayed up, contemplating what she had said.

I agreed with her and didn't desire marital conflict over any spiritual experience. At least once or twice a week, I would begin to stay at the farm after feeding the cows to pray, read Scripture, and seek this spiritual gift. After several attempts, I laid back against the pickup seat one night, listening to "Adoration" by Mike Adkins. As I relaxed and softly sang the words of his song, I heard him sing in a heavenly language. I felt something gently put pressure on my throat. I opened my mouth and began to speak in a language that I did not understand. I began to experience a personal prayer language all my own. I was not overcome with emotion or exhilaration. I heard no bells ringing. The ground didn't shake, nor did the trees fall over. I spoke in this unknown language for at least thirty minutes.

I do not know whether or not everyone should have this experience, but for me, this experience was confirmation about God's presence and that GOD IS REAL! Even though I had been a pastor and attended seminary, I did not know that God was real and personal like I was experiencing. Even though I had my dramatic encounter with Anna, my sister in Christ in the street, my concept of God was still more intellectual than personal. Transformation of the mind and heart is not a simple task. I had grown up in the church, been baptized, had done all the right things, functioned as a pastor better than most, could pray inspiring prayers, had been a tither from childhood; but I didn't know that God was alive and personal as I had recently encountered Him. I have to confess that I had once mocked the old hymn, "In the Garden." I thought it was a nice, sentimental song, but how could anyone walk and talk with the Lord? Now I was slowly beginning to understand that it was possible this songwriter had written these lyrics from his own personal experience. I was beginning to change from not worrying about what other people might think to experiencing a "real Jesus."

My spiritual growth, desire, and determination grew stronger. I became a reflection of the description that the Psalmist wrote generations ago: *"As the deer pants for streams of water, so my soul pants for you, O God. My soul thirsts for God, for the living God. When can I go and meet with God?" (Psalm 42:1-2).* I became convinced in my spirit that I was supposed to attend a Thanksgiving Convocation in Houston that year instead of going home for the holidays. Needless to say, my decision didn't please my wife, who was just as determined to be with her family's Thanksgiving reunion and later to visit my parents with the grandchildren before returning. A common question began to be raised: "What's going on? Does he think he's a preacher again?" In all honesty, I didn't understand my behavior either. I desired to be with family over the holidays, but reverential fear of the Lord and His desire overcame any personal wishes. I said goodbye to the family as they departed. My wife was still an unhappy camper with me. It was difficult to go separate ways, but Houston, here I come.

Many speakers there exposed me to biblical truth and understanding that I had not heard before. On the last day of the meeting, after sitting all morning listening to speakers from 8 am to about 3 pm, my tailbone was numb, and I was half dozing. I was sitting by myself midway to the rear of the auditorium when suddenly someone slapped me on the back. Thinking it might be someone I knew, I quickly came to my senses and turned around to see who was there. No one was within 30 feet of me. *That was odd,* I thought. *Did I dream I was slapped on the back?* I turned around and tried to refocus on the speaker, but I soon began to doze again when I was slapped on my back once more. This time, however, it was like someone helped me to my feet. I found myself suddenly walking very fast to the altar kneeling in front of the speaker. I began to weep uncontrollably as I knelt. Weeping was unusual for me; I often prided myself for not crying while attending the saddest movie. I was also weeping without knowing why. Looking up with tears rolling down my face, I saw the speaker watching me. Refocusing, my eyes shifted to the ceiling, where an opening the size of a small window suddenly appeared. It was like seeing a beautiful painting, except what I witnessed was moving! An indescribable blue with white streaks like angel hair was swirling at the same time. The blue was the bluest that I had ever seen, before or since. Then I felt an unseen presence engulf me in an atmosphere of peace and love. I became oblivious to my surroundings. It was a surreal moment as if an actual person was in front and behind me with arms around me at the same time. I felt God love this rascal like I'd never felt love before. His presence was so real that I felt He was holding me as I knelt at the altar weeping. His love was so overpowering and complete. All my guilt, shame, sin, failure, frustration, and stress were being released simultaneously while receiving a love that was forgiving, restoring, and encouraging at the same time.

After the service, I felt the Lord tell me in my spirit to write letters to all my family, telling them what I had experienced in the last six months. I asked God, "Who is family?" Then I grabbed a handful of pamphlets from one speaker. After returning home, I discovered I had picked up 26 booklets. I ended up writing 26 letters to family members. As time progressed, I found that this letter was prophetic concerning my wife's family and my family as to what would happen over the ensuing years. The letter stressed that every person should become rooted in faith; so they would be able to endure and be victorious over every hardship they would face, even the death of loved ones.

I wrote this letter out of obedience regardless of what they might think. I am quite honest in saying that just because I was excited about discovering God in a new and exciting way, no one else really cared. In fact, it created more problems in the family than it solved. I confess that some of my words, actions, and difficult business decisions may have turned off some people to Jesus. I was bold and straightforward, and my heart was in the right place, but as some of them rejected me, they also rejected the Jesus in me. That is not at all what I hoped to have accomplished. We have still not solved all of our problems, and this testimony with my family is still being written. I know more today than I did yesterday, and I will know more tomorrow because of the grace of God that He continues to give. Nothing would deter me from continuing to discover my newfound faith in God. The Scripture became alive in a way that I had not known before. New knowledge and revelation were being gleaned from its pages. Nita, however, confronted me at supper one evening that I had become a hermit who had separated himself from family. Somehow, I needed to find balance and spend time with her and the children. Due to her urging, I came out of my closet for the next couple of weeks and sat down in my favorite recliner to spend quality time with them. The vast majority of the time was spent watching television with no words being spoken. I'm not sure we were communicating and having quality time, but we were sitting together. The children did enjoy my helping them with their homework, especially math. It was difficult for me to balance my hunger for spiritual understanding with my desire for quality family time. Both were important, but striking a balance was more difficult than I thought possible.

I began to discover a practical Jesus who is concerned about you as a person, about your life, your needs, your desires, problems, and your family. It's about learning how to become a companion with Jesus and how Jesus becomes a companion with you. For example, one Monday morning, I received a letter from a district highway department that informed me that I was going to have to move my bulk agency; because they were going to build an overpass over the railroad tracks. My plant would be directly underneath. Picking up the telephone, I called

I BEGAN TO DISCOVER A PRACTICAL JESUS WHO IS CONCERNED ABOUT YOU AS A PERSON ...

the gentleman who had sent the letter. I began to get a sinking feeling in the pit of my stomach as he informed me that there would be no government assistance to help move my business. It was easy to understand the reasoning for relocating. It would be a hazardous situation to be loading a gasoline transport below with a driver discarding a lighted cigarette from a vehicle above. The possibility of an explosion would be devastating.

When my wife came to work that afternoon, I told her that I needed to see our banker who helped us begin this business. Though I had been faithful in making timely monthly payments, he told me what I knew all along—he would be unable to loan me any additional funds because I didn't have any additional collateral that I could offer the bank in return for a loan. He did arrange for me to see the bank owner, who happened to be there that afternoon. This retired gentleman had worked in higher levels of state and national government earlier in his career. Telling him of my situation, I inquired if he knew of anyone who could help in this situation. He showed genuine empathy for my problem but said he didn't know how he would be able to help. I thanked him for his time and went back to the office.

Showing my wife, the letter she inquired, "What can we do?"

"I don't know," I shrugged and related my conversations at the bank. This was a situation that I could not control or do something about. Retreating to my prayer closet that evening; I remembered a speaker at the Thanksgiving Convocation whose primary emphasis was declaring Scripture to God concerning any circumstance. I hadn't been too impressed with his position; because I remembered past parishioners who declared Scriptures for various situations with mixed results. Some were successful, but some weren't. My faith at this time was about as small as a mustard seed. I decided to trust and believe as best I could in my newfound scriptural knowledge. I thought, *What do I have to lose?*

Two principles found in Scripture became key for me:

1. God gives life to the dead, and He calls things that are not as though they were.
2. God has the power to do what He has promised.[1]

Morning and night, I began to call what was not as though it were—I declared that my wholesale business would move to a new location without cost to me and spoke that God had the power to do what He had promised. I received more letters, and the deadline to relocate was fast approaching. I could do nothing else but continue to praise God and make my petition to Him. I had no other remedy.

About one week before the deadline, a stranger appeared in my office. He introduced himself as the district engineer who had been writing me the letters. We had conversed on the phone on a few occasions. As he introduced himself, I couldn't understand why he was smiling. I was envisioning the end was near and thought to myself, *this guy is pretty insensitive.*

He said, "You really have influence in high places—especially in the state of Texas."

Very surprised, I replied, "I'm afraid I don't know what you're talking about."

I could tell by the look on his face that he didn't believe me; he thought I was pulling his leg. "You've got to be kidding me," he replied.

I repeated, "What are you talking about?"

"Well," he answered, "my supervisor got a phone call from a representative of Santa Fe Railroad the other day. He said that if we didn't take care of the gentleman in that east Texas town where the overpass was to be built, they would not allow the state of Texas to cross over the railroad tracks!"

My emotions erupted as I shouted, "Praise the Lord!"

That shocked me more than it did my visitor. He just shrugged his shoulders and said, "You gotta tell me, *who* do you know?"

"Sir," I replied, "I don't know anyone, but I'm trying to know Jesus. This is a miracle!"

He shook his head and told me, "In my 40 years with the Texas Highway Department, Santa Fe had never refused their request to cross over their tracks anywhere in the state. That's good news for you because the state will pay all your moving costs. You forward all the invoices to me, and I'll pass them to the right department to see they get paid."

Suddenly my legs felt weak as he left. I sat down, and tears erupted in relief and overwhelming joy—all while being in shock. Unbelievable. *Wow!* I praised God for the next few minutes. If I had not received that assistance, my business would've closed. The land that my business relocated upon became the collateral for the additional financial assistance that was needed.

My prayers continued to reflect thanksgiving and praise. I briefly wondered whether the bank owner did have some great influence that he had denied or whether God had used him on my behalf. For me, either way, it was a miracle! I didn't care how it came about, only that it did! My faith, the size of a mustard seed, increased dramatically. In this one instance where I had felt no hope, had no answer, or remedy other than Scripture, my earnestness, pleading, perseverance, and spiritual demeanor were focused wholly upon the Lord. I discovered that when I humbly turned my problem over to God, believing in my heart that what His Word says is true, and without doubt, I allowed God to act in His way and His timing (rather than try to manipulate the outcome), His hand was at work for my good in every situation. Scripture instructed that I was to seek first God's kingdom and His righteousness and promised that when I did, **all these things** would be given to me as well. His Word promised I did not need to worry about tomorrow because tomorrow would worry about itself. Each day would have enough trouble of its own.[2] This outcome with my business bore witness to His truth! It was a testimony to a covenant relationship, a two-way relationship. I've heard people say that if you confess whatever you desire, it will be given unto you. For example, a new car. I don't believe that. There seems to be a subtle distinction between confessing perhaps a selfish desire over a circumstance that affects the survival of oneself and family; I'm not sure that I really have the answer on this subject; because I've had other serious situations where unselfish desires I prayed were not acted upon. However, I believe that if any person gets his life right with God, gets his heart right in faith with the Lord Jesus, and his prayer is in accordance with God's Will, it will be done. John said it like this:

"This is the confidence we have in approaching God: that if we ask anything according to his will, he hears us. And if we know that he hears us—whatever we ask—we know that we have what we asked of him."[3]

The key for God acting on our behalf in prayer may rest upon our petition being in accordance with His Will. In all things, we must trust His sovereignty. God answers every prayer, even if His answer is no or not now, or He answers us in a way that

23

may not make sense at the time. God knows our end from our beginning.[4] He stands outside of time, and He has promised to work all things together for our good because we love Him and are called according to His purpose.[5] God's faithfulness to answer my prayers for my business was just the start. Unbeknownst to me, God was just beginning to intervene in my journey; and that is **Hope Beyond**!

ENDNOTES

1. Romans 4:16-21.
2. Matthew 6:33-34.
3. 1 John 5:14-15.
4. Isaiah 46:10.
5. Romans 8:28.

CHAPTER 3

GOD'S SENSE OF HUMOR

A backfiring car drew my attention as I paused from what I was doing. My business had been relocated on the main highway, so the noise wasn't unusual. What was unusual, however, was to see an older, yellow Volkswagen Beetle driving up the road. Black smoke followed it with another backfire. The way it sounded and looked, it needed at least a ring job or possibly a complete overhaul.

My office was an inside glass enclosure, where depending on the reflection, a person in the office might see me or might not. Three female employees worked in an open area, each with an individual desk and no partitions separating them. Everyone liked this arrangement as it allowed for informal social contact while working together. The outside walls of the building were constructed with tinted glass windows where no one could see inside during the day.

All eyes were focused on the Volkswagen that came to a stop outside our front door. A man, who looked like the TV character Grizzly Adams, stepped out of the car.

I don't know how he could even ride in it. He was at least 6 foot 6, weighed between 250 to 300 pounds, and had long hair and a beard. He walked inside to the five-foot-tall reception desk with a countertop and teller opening. This desk became a room divider, which separated customers from employees. Looking around briefly while closing his big fist, he began to pound on the countertop declaring in a loud voice for all to hear, "God sent me here to save somebody's soul. Who is it?"

As soon as I heard what he said, I knew that he was there for me. I wanted to hide under my desk and not come out. The employee who worked right in front of me was staring at me even though she couldn't see me through the one-way window. I could read her lips moving slowly, saying,

"Get out here, boss!"

What was probably only a minute or less seemed like an eternity. The man at the reception desk clenched his fists again, raising his voice several octaves as he pounded the countertop, shouting, "God sent me here to save somebody's soul. I know I heard Him correctly. I'm not leaving until whoever it is comes out!"

With that declaration, all three of my employees got up in unison and shouted, "See you, tomorrow boss—we're leaving!"

I arose from my desk and walked out with a nonchalant demeanor, saying, "I don't know who you are, sir, but if you will join me outside, we will not disturb the business or customers."

We walked outside another front entrance and sat on the steps. Immediately, I began to weep uncontrollably, just as I had done with Anna, the lady in the street. This was unusual behavior for me and far from my understanding. Gaining control, I began to relay to this man, my recent experience with Anna. Before I knew it, I had given this total stranger a quick synopsis of having been a pastor, resigning the pulpit, working for a major oil company, and coming into this East Texas town to begin my own business. This hulk of a man looked down on me with a smile on his face and asked, "Little brother, do you know what a deliverance ministry is?"

"No," I replied. "I have never heard of a deliverance pastor or ministry. What is it?"

He began to explain that God calls individuals into deliverance ministry. The basis of that ministry focuses entirely on the Gospel of Mark. More than the other three Gospels, Mark relates how Jesus delivered people from demonic and unclean spirits. The stranger continued that he would be the first to admit that most Christian believers had never heard of this type of ministry. Also, the vast majority of Christians would probably not want to understand this ministry either. We talked for a bit longer. He introduced himself as Dustin and told me that he lived close to the lake, about 25 miles away. As we continued to talk, he had a warmth about him that relaxed me. Any anxiety and nervousness I felt disappeared. As he began to go into further detail about his ministry, I suddenly began to laugh. He looked at me as if thinking, *"I didn't think I said anything funny, so why are you laughing?"*

"Forgive me," I said, "I mean no disrespect to what you were telling me, but suddenly I realized that the Lord has a sense of humor."

He nodded his head in agreement.

"The thought entered my mind as you were talking," I continued, "that I attended the most liberal theological seminary in the country during the mid-'60s. Your deliverance ministry is probably the farthest right possible on the religious scale as the seminary I attended was the farthest left."

"Yes," he replied, "most seminaries, denominations, churches, and Christians believe today that signs, wonders, miracles, and deliverance ended with Jesus and His disciples during the first century AD." Glancing at his watch and rising to leave, Dustin said to me, "Little brother, it's late. We'll talk again. I'm presently holding a meeting on the lake this Saturday at 7:00 pm. I believe the Lord is telling me in my spirit that you're to be there. I don't think that He is calling you into the deliverance ministry, but I sense that God is trying to expose you to the workings of His Holy Spirit. Here are the directions."

I SENSE GOD IS TRYING TO EXPOSE YOU TO THE WORKINGS OF HIS HOLY SPIRIT.

He put his hand on my shoulder and held out the other one for me to shake and said, "So, can I expect to see you there?"

"Yes," I shook his hand, "I'll be there."

He offered a word of prayer for me and left.

I remained at the office for a few minutes contemplating our conversation together. *Wow!* I thought, *it's pretty amazing that no other customers came on a busy mid-afternoon from around 3:00 pm until closing at 5:30 pm.* The telephone was silent as well. Another strange experience and encounter. I halfway wished that I had told him that I wouldn't be there. *What would my customers think if they knew I was associating with a person who claimed a ministry of healing people from unclean and demonic spirits?* My newfound sense of reverent fear of God overcame any objections.

Saturday evening came quickly. As I parked the pickup where the meeting would occur, those feelings of anxiety returned. Looking around, I breathed a sigh of relief. No one was there yet. My mind thought back to the events and unusual spiritual encounters of recent days. I was somewhat curious to see what might occur at this meeting tonight. I was still hoping not to see anyone I knew at this meeting for fear of social rejection and customer reprisal. Dustin arrived, and I got out of my pickup, determined to see this meeting through. Trying not to be noticed, I sat in a corner at the rear of the room. I went out of my way not to be social with those who attended.

After delivering a brief message, Dustin invited those who desired prayer to come forward one at a time. A woman went forward, but I couldn't hear what she whispered in Dustin's ear. She was sitting in a chair in front of him. He began to declare words of Scripture over her. He then commanded an unclean spirit to depart from her in the name of Jesus. She reacted with tears, trembling, and repeating the words that he told her to say. This act of deliverance lasted about 20 minutes with this lady. When it ended, he gave her the opportunity to speak to the audience. She simply said that as he prayed and commanded unclean spirits to leave, she felt as if a huge weight had been lifted from her. She further stated that she felt a strong presence of God's love and peace envelop her.

Over the next couple of months, I continued to attend Dustin's meetings and began to appreciate this type of ministry. It was easy to see that the recipients were receiving whatever they needed from the Lord by the power of His Holy Spirit. I didn't really understand all that was going on, but it didn't matter to me at this time.

What mattered was hearing a person testify what they believed they had received from the Lord. What mattered was actually witnessing a person act differently from being set free from the bondage they felt engulfed them. What was paramount to my understanding was discovering that God's Word and Holy Spirit were the same today as they were in the first century. This truth began a building block for my faith and for **Hope Beyond.**

CHAPTER 4

AN ELECTRIFYING MOMENT

The moment was silent as I sat in my office. It was a windy, cool, and sunny mid-January day. Wow—it was hard to believe that almost two years had passed since I had met Anna in the street! It had been about 13 months since my deliverance buddy, Dustin, had shown up unexpectedly at the business. Since then, I had attended every meeting where he ministered.

The workings of the Holy Spirit did not frighten me anymore, but my reverent fear of the Lord continued. He was the one responsible for what I was seeing. What I read in Scripture was sometimes manifested in front of my eyes. I could not deny what I was seeing. As I continued to read various authors and search the Scriptures, coupled with the results of deliverance ministry, I was gaining exposure to new spiritual insight, knowledge, and understanding. All of this was foreign to my traditional and mainline denominational upbringing and theological understanding.

One of my employees greeted me, interrupting my thoughts as he placed my personal mail on the desk. I picked up the monthly newsletter from the Full Gospel Business Men's Fellowship. It highlighted mission trips being planned throughout 1983 and 1984. I began to read about a Florida men's chapter that was going to Venezuela for ten days. Suddenly, my chair felt as if electricity was running through it and flowing through me from head to toe. Instantly, I knew that I was going! I reread the article, jotting down the name and phone number of the man in Miami, Florida, who was organizing the trip. Without hesitation, I called him immediately. I don't know why I was surprised when he answered. Maybe I was hoping he wouldn't. I was beginning to feel queasy in my stomach. His friendliness helped to relieve my anxiety. I briefly introduced myself and told him that I would like to join his group going to Venezuela if there was still an opening.

"Son," he said, "I have been trying to fill that one remaining spot for two weeks. Your calling is not an accident but a divine appointment. Praise God! I am delighted to have you join us Floridians and three other Texans! I will mail your instructions, flight schedules, and itinerary today."

Reality began to sink in as I hung up the telephone. *What have I done?* That queasy feeling began to come back into my stomach. My legs felt weak. My hands were trembling slightly as I thought about what had just happened.

I wasn't looking forward to telling my wife what I had done. Nita still wasn't on board with this Holy Spirit "stuff." She was happy just going to church on Sunday with the children and me, seeing our friends, and eating Sunday lunch with them. Our discussion did not go well, to say the least. She voiced her objections to what I was doing and refused to participate in any of it. Nita added a threat this time, something she had not said before: "If you continue in this and go to Venezuela, there will be a divorce in this family after you get back."

With that being said, she stormed into the bedroom and told me to sleep on the couch.

The queasy feeling returned, but it now gave way to a different sickening feeling that I had never felt before. It was certainly not my heartfelt desire to have any family arguments, but her threat of divorce was devastating. *Did she really mean it? Could a marriage end so easily after twenty-two years?*

Lying on the couch, I closed my eyes and began to pray silently.

"What am I to do, Lord? I am convinced that you're calling me to go on this mission trip; yet, I do not want to lose my wife or family in the process."

A minute or two passed. Suddenly, a Scripture came to mind. Turning in my Bible, I began to read:

> *"Do not suppose that I come to bring peace to the earth. I did not come to bring peace, but a sword. For I have come to turn 'a man against his father, a daughter against her mother, a daughter-in-law against her mother-in-law – a man's enemies will be the members of his own household.' Anyone who loves his father or mother more than me is not worthy of me; anyone who loves his son or daughter more than me is not worthy of me; anyone who does not take his cross and follow me is not worthy of me. Whoever finds his life will lose it, and whoever loses his life for my sake will find it."*[1]

"Wow! Those are harsh sounding words, Lord," I whispered.

I continued to reflect upon what Nita had said and what I had just read. Somehow, I could not believe that the Lord would allow a family to endure divorce as a cost to do ministry in His name. Yet, I knew that every person had a free will and could make whatever choices they desired. Wasn't that one fateful result of Adam and Eve's decision in the garden?

Then I reasoned in my mind that if God could orchestrate a woman in the street, a stranger showing up at my business, and my office chair feeling electrified, then He could handle my wife. *Didn't I believe that God was all-sufficient and all-powerful?* "Yes, God," I breathed, "I will obey You and go. I will trust You to take care of my family situation."

I slipped to my knees and prayed aloud, "God, I give Nita to you for the preservation of our love and family. I am convinced that You have called me to Venezuela. There will be no divorce, only unity in Jesus' name. Amen."

Gradually, awareness began to arise within as I realized that the queasy, sickening feeling I had experienced was being replaced with calmness settling over my mind and spirit.

Attempting to find a comfortable spot on the couch, I fell asleep.

ENDNOTE
1. Matthew 10:34-39.

CHAPTER 5

JOURNEY TO "THE LAND OF GRACE"

March 15, 1984—the day of departure to Venezuela had arrived. I was truly thankful that my wife had helped me pack the suitcase and load everything in the pickup the night before. The children seemed to be as excited about my going as I was. Perhaps their excitement was due more to the activities that Nita had planned for them. Kissing everyone goodbye, I drove away with emotions of anxiety, anticipation, and excitement while giving thanks to God that my wife had not spoken about her threat again. Praise God, an answer to my prayer!

I had previously read that Christopher Columbus had nicknamed Venezuela "the land of grace," based upon its natural beauty and landscape. It would be no accident that I would discover the grace of God in so many different and amazing ways within this "land of grace."

I had driven less than five miles out of town when suddenly my body began to sweat profusely. At the same time, I was feeling sick to my stomach. *How could I be feeling so good one minute and so bad the next? Was I burning up with fever?* I looked at my watch to determine if I could find my doctor and still have time to catch my flight out of Houston. Turning around, I quickly drove to his office. Of course, it was his day off! His nurse did tell me, however, that he might be at the hospital making early visits to his patients. Determined to find him, I drove three blocks to the hospital, and as I walked into the main corridor, there he was. Hallelujah! After our greeting, I told him that I was flying out of the country when suddenly I felt ill with a high fever just as I was leaving town. He said to give him 15 minutes and directed me to wait in an empty room. About five minutes later, a nurse came in, took my vitals, and said, "Your temperature and blood pressure are completely normal. Why are you here?"

"Well," I replied, "I was sweating profusely and felt sick to my stomach."

She checked the blood pressure cuff once more and shook her head, "Your temperature and blood pressure are as normal as you are feeling abnormal."

With that remark, the nurse seemed agitated as she left the room as if I was there merely to waste her time. My doctor arrived within five minutes and inquired, "What have you done to my nurse?"

"Doc, I don't know what's going with this sweating and feeling sick at my stomach."

"Well, perhaps it's only a case of nerves about the unknown," he replied.

He felt around, looked in my throat, listened to my heart and lungs, and said, "Everything looks good and sounds normal; I find nothing wrong with you, so go enjoy your adventure. You're probably having a case of nerves about the trip."

Sixty-eight dollars later, I left the hospital feeling just as hot as when I went in. In some ways, I felt even hotter.

Relieved, however, I drove again towards Houston. About ten miles from town, I suddenly felt something that I had never experienced before. It was like a weight being lifted from my shoulders. The feeling was similar to wearing a heavy coat and then removing it. Later, other believers who heard me relay this experience would tell me that I had been deceived and attacked by an evil spirit. Upon hearing this, my mind thought back to the early testimonies I had heard at those deliverance services. Such an experience, however, was still foreign to my understanding.

I glanced at my watch and saw that I had to hurry if I was to make my flight. It would be close. Thankfully, I made no wrong turns and took the correct exits to the airport. I drove into the first parking lot available while noticing an airport van out front preparing to leave. I was hoping to be able to make it. I drove up to the closed gate when a sign suddenly flashed, "The lot is full." *What was I to do?* I had no choice but to back up and try to find another place. Just then, the gate began to open even though the sign was still flashing, "The lot is full." I quickly drove through the gate, hoping I would find a parking place inside. I had only gone about 45 feet when a vacant spot appeared. Praise the Lord! Pulling into the spot, I quickly grabbed my bags and ran to the front, hoping that the airport van had not left. As I rounded the corner, the van driver was standing outside and began to wave me forward.

As I was approaching, he said, "I saw you coming and decided to wait for you!"

"Thank you so much!" I responded. "You saved me from missing my flight!"

Departing at the proper terminal, I told the driver again how much I appreciated his waiting for me.

"Be blessed," I said and gave him a generous tip. "I haven't had such courtesy since I have been flying."

Thankfully, I had time to grab a quick snack and drink on the way to the departure gate. There I would meet and join three other Texans flying to meet our Floridian brothers in Miami. Based on the number of people already sitting at the gate, it would be a full flight. Looking around, I could not determine who my fellow travelers might be. It was about twenty minutes to board when my name and three others were called to the main desk. A state director of our Fellowship from Midland, Texas, had gathered us together right before the flight. Since it was so close to boarding time, the attendant told us to board our party. Though we purchased our tickets individually, we discovered that all of us were sitting 2x2 beside each other.

As I was relaxing and beginning to get acquainted with my new Christian brothers, my mind was also remembering the day's events. It'd been an adventure, to say the least. I had experienced some sort of spiritual attack or enemy deception. An empty parking spot was available even though the gate sign flashed, "The lot is full," when the gate suddenly opened. An airport van driver seemed to be waiting just for me at just the right time. Four strangers meeting for the flight discovered assigned seats sitting side-by-side. No person could plan a trip any better than that! Everything I needed was there at just the right time and place. *How amazing was that? Was this a mere coincidence?*

The four of us arrived on time at the busy Miami Airport. We proceeded to the area where we would ride the tram to the terminal where the international flights would depart. As we waited for about five minutes, a couple appeared that our state director knew from Arizona. They were supposed to have been in Miami two hours earlier, but their flight had been delayed. A few minutes later, another couple joining us from Georgia arrived at the tram with a similar story. Here were three groups of fellow travelers meeting unplanned within ten minutes of each other at the busy Miami Airport to take the same airport tram to our departure gate. The odds of that happening are astronomical! *Again, mere coincidence?* I don't think so. I had no sooner sat down for the tram ride when a Scripture came to my mind:

> *"He will tend his flock like a shepherd; he will gather the lambs in his arms; he will carry them in his bosom, and gently lead those that are with young."[1]*

My newfound roommate and partner in ministry continued to sit together on our flights to Maracaibo and then to Caracas. An Argentinian woman, about 55 years of age, boarded and sat in a vacant seat behind us with another mission teammate on this one-hour ten-minute trip. About halfway into the flight, my attention turned to the conversation behind us as I heard our teammate leading this woman to salvation in Jesus. I was overwhelmed by this event and by his boldness.

Unbelievable! I thought, *out of 100 empty seats on this flight, this lady "happened" to sit down by the only Spanish-speaking member of our group who had lived a part of his life in Argentina and who understood her dialect! Another mere coincidence?* I don't think so! I did not fully realize it yet, but I was being exposed to a God who orchestrates time, people, and events to bring His will to earth.

JESUS WAS REVEALING HIMSELF TO ME IN A WAY THAT WAS NEW, REAL, PRACTICAL, AND PERSONAL.

Jesus was revealing Himself to me in a way that was new, real, practical, and personal. I had gone to church for as long as I could remember and worshipped in the tradition in which I was raised. Though I had a theological degree, I confess that my concept of God was similar to someone who was just "out there." I was beginning to awaken to an understanding of God, the Father, who was caring, loving, and alive. Now, God was becoming my Father, manifesting His love in a way that was real and personal as a friend. It was exciting to be in this type of atmosphere!

This day had revealed more about my understanding of God's nature than I had understood for a lifetime. Here was a practical Jesus being similar to a good Shepherd gathering His flock. I was discovering and participating in an aspect of God's grace that allowed me to partner with Him in bringing His will to earth as it is in the heavens. I didn't fully understand it at that time, and still today cannot comprehend fully such an undertaking; however, it was and is wonderful to be a recipient and a partaker of His grace.

The plane landed in Venezuela. The day had been long as we arrived in Caracas at the hotel around 9:00 pm. I was so excited and overwhelmed that I had already discovered facets of God's grace before unknown to me. I did not know it yet, but my journey to the "Land of Grace" would continue to bring unexplainable— but undeniable—aspects of God's love. I could hardly wait for the sunrise!

ENDNOTE

1. Isaiah 40:11 ESV.

CHAPTER 6

God's Perfect Love

The next morning, my roommate Andrew and I joined other teammates at breakfast. We began to share what God had done for each participant in getting here. We grew in excitement and anticipation about what God desired to accomplish through us on this mission trip. I ordered coffee. To my surprise, they brought a very small cup. Then they filled the cup half full. The waiter said something in Spanish that none of us understood. I shrugged my shoulders as he pointed at the cup. Yes, I nodded. He filled the rest of the cup with milk. About that time, two members of our team, Victor, a retired general, and his wife, Candace, walked up. Candace explained to us that their coffee was very strong. We should always drink it half-and-half with milk. She was right. It was very strong! I could instantly feel the caffeine awaken my entire body!

This day was spent relaxing, touring the city, and getting ready for the first banquet that night at the hotel. Even though it was supposed to begin at 8:00 pm, we learned later that we would probably start closer to 9:00 pm. It seemed that the main event always began one hour after the time it was scheduled.

I heard an amazing testimony that night from Victor. A highly respected retired general, Victor had been Commander of NATO forces at one time in his career. He testified how his WWII Corsair airplane had literally been shot out from under him in combat. None of his controls worked. He could see antiaircraft holes everywhere in the aircraft. Victor thought this was the end. He knew that without controls, he would not be able to ditch safely into the ocean. As he continued to fly, Victor remembered how it felt—as if someone or some unseen force—lifted and steadied the airplane. Seeing a small island in the distance but without any ability to fly the plane, his aircraft began to descend on its own. Landing perfectly in the water close to land, he got out safely and quickly swam to shore. Victor was soon rescued. *Wow! Wow! Wow! What an amazing miracle!*

After Victor's testimony, his wife Candace asked me to stand with her as she ministered to those who had come forward for prayers. She instructed me to stand behind whoever she was praying with. It was my job to catch them if they fell under the power of the Holy Spirit. She prayed over one lady who walked to us stooped over with a cane. The lady was healed instantly by the power of the Holy Spirit! She was able to return to her seat, walking upright and normally *without* a cane. I watched Candace intently during this time and felt God was instructing me on how to minister and pray for people. I watched this beautiful servant of God minister so effectively with the power of the Holy Spirit. Her voice was normal, comforting, and peaceful.

A team meeting was held after breakfast on Saturday morning. Three teams had been assigned to go to house churches to offer their testimonies and serve the people in whatever capacity was needed. The rest of us had free time until the evening banquet. I confess that I was very disappointed that I would not be part of a team, not even as an observer. After lunch, my roommate and I continued to lounge around the hotel and shop for our families. Five or six of us gathered around 3:00 pm in the lobby lounge and continued to visit. One of the team planners excitedly burst upon the scene—he had just received the fourth request for a team to come to a house church at 4:00 pm. As he described this request, my skin became electrified, just as it had been when I read about this trip in the newsletter. As soon as he quit speaking, I jumped up, volunteering my roommate and me to be the team. Choosing us, he told us that two women would be out front of the hotel at 4:00 pm to take us to the meeting place. Andrew and I quickly went to our room to prepare for the meeting. I was overjoyed to be on this assignment, believing this was God's will.

Sure enough, precisely at 4:00 pm, our host drove up to the front of the hotel. Thankfully, one of them spoke some English. We introduced ourselves. Our hosts, Bethany and Ruth, assured us that an interpreter would be at the house as we spoke. They told us they'd been believers in Christ for many years. In fact, Bethany had led our student interpreter to Christ and trained her. Together, they had started this house church in Bethany's home.

As we drove to her house, I could not help noticing that people lived in either extreme poverty or extreme wealth. Several hillsides were filled with people living in boxes, big plastic containers, or makeshift lean-tos. Garbage was thrown outside to be washed away whenever the rains came. It was a sad situation to look upon.

We arrived at a nice home, a typical Spanish hacienda with a courtyard and lovely surroundings. Led by a college-age girl and boy playing guitars, the group was singing as we walked in. They stopped and warmly greeted us with handshakes and hugs. A couple of women had pre-teenage children with them. The college-age girl, Kemena, was our interpreter.

Andrew spoke first. I highly respected the spiritual experiences he had already shared. My Christian love for my roommate began almost immediately. Andrew's actions and words reflected his spiritual maturity and understanding. God had been so kind to place me with such a knowledgeable servant of healing ministry. As he concluded his testimony, he asked the group if there were any particular prayer needs. Then, I would speak.

Kemena immediately spoke out, requesting prayer for her back. She explained first to us in English, then in Spanish to the group, that she had been in a car accident about a year earlier, causing damage to her spine. Surgery had not corrected the issues. She still had problems with one foot and complications with one leg now an inch and a half shorter than the other. She was in constant pain. Andrew instructed her to lay flat on her back on the floor. He placed his hands underneath her shoulders. He then instructed me to place my hands underneath her feet. He told me to pray silently for him and her healing. He began to pray specifically about her back condition. Suddenly I felt a jolt, then a hard slap on my back that made me drop her feet as I fell forward towards the girl. Only a quick reaction kept me from falling on top of her. I felt embarrassed. I quickly straightened up as the young girl and Andrew were rising to their feet. The girl was excited and told the group that her pain had left her body as Andrew prayed. She turned to me and said that her pain ended when she felt me pull her legs and feet. Since I hadn't done anything, I didn't know what to say to her, only, "Praise the Lord!"

While the group joined Kemena and Andrew with shouts of joy and rejoicing over her instant miracle, my thoughts returned to the hard, back slap that I had received at the Thanksgiving Convocation previously attended. I believe this was the work of an angel, though I had never seen one.

Andrew turned the program over to me. I gave my brief testimony emphasizing God's love. It was still inconceivable that He loved this "rascal" enough to send His messenger—"the Lady in the Street"—to get my life reconnected to Him. If God would do that for me, He would do that for anyone.

> *"Peter said, 'Now I know for certain that God doesn't show favoritism with people but treats everyone on the same basis.'"*[1]

As I closed my testimony, I followed Andrew's lead in asking the group if anyone had prayer concerns. Bethany, the host of this house church, spoke a prophetic word over Andrew, telling him, "The Lord has called you from the beginning and given you the gift of healing. This has been confirmed to you many times as you prayed for others. The Lord will continue to use you in this ministry, for you have been a faithful and obedient ambassador of Christ and have accomplished much. I will enlarge your tent, and you will accomplish greater works for Me, saith the Lord."

She paused for a moment as she gazed at me and began to prophesy, saying, "The Lord is pleased that you answered His call to come to Venezuela. Due to turning your ear and heart again unto the Lord with earnestness, God is giving you the gift of prophecy. You will be able to discern spirits—to discern what is troubling others. Knowledge will come forth that will release the burdens of the people, unlocking their hearts. The Holy Spirit will come and heal them. In My name and by the Holy Spirit, words of wisdom and knowledge will be given to you to instruct them. Praise My holy name for the name of Jesus is above every name. The Lord also says your time and season is not yet come but that it will soon. You will be used greatly in speaking before people, in being a prophet, and as a healer of the Spirit."

When she finished speaking, what felt like a hand upon my head turned my head to a particular lady in the room. I saw in my mind words printed on a ticker tape as my mouth opened. I spoke these words to the lady. It was like being in a semi-trance, yet I was conscious of what I was doing. As my words were interpreted into Spanish for her, the woman began crying. Remaining in my place, I watched the interpreter move towards the lady and speak with her. The lady expressed emotions of anger, shame, and hurt from her husband, who had recently divorced her.

Andrew and I both offered prayers for her as we felt led by the Holy Spirit. It's difficult to explain the heavy presence of the Holy Spirit that I felt at this time. When we had finished praying, the Spirit of the Lord caused me to focus on another lady in the group. God's power through the Holy Spirit produced similar results. Everything happening resulted from the outpouring of God's love following the prophetic word that had been given. Andrew and I continued to follow the leading of the Holy Spirit as we ministered to the various needs within the group.

To me, it was becoming evident that the presence and power of God were manifesting before our eyes in a manner that I had never known or thought possible. This was the Holy Spirit of God at work in the 20th century as written about by His early disciples. I was amazed, overwhelmed, and marveled at how the Holy

Spirit correlated this tag-team ministry between Andrew and me for everyone's needs. Touching my mouth, as if to confirm this moment was real, I was spell-bound how the Spirit of God gave me various words of knowledge and revelation about the needs of these people. Speaking God's prophetic word for their underlying concern would begin a conversation drawing out their deeper hurts. This was often witnessed by their bursting forth with crying and sharing their needs unashamedly. The Spirit of God provided Andrew and me alternate words of knowledge and revelation for that person's needs. Finishing each time, we witnessed smiles on their faces. They had felt God's presence in a special way. Everyone would testify that their burdens had lifted and that they had been healed in Jesus' name. *Amazing—just amazing!*

This experience was what I had always dreamed ministry to be—a true reflection of what is written in God's Word—to become a vessel for God's outpouring of His grace and a conduit for the power of His Holy Spirit manifesting in signs, wonders, and miracles. This was awakening my pastor's heart for service again. I was discovering a God who orchestrated time, people, and events to bring about His love for others and to bring His will to earth. Simply, God was displaying His love for others. These experiences were the birth of this book, **Hope Beyond!**

After about an hour of further prayer and ministry, the Spirit of God subsided. We sang a song and took a break. It had been an intense session. I welcomed time to reflect upon everything that had happened. Needless to say, my emotions continued in a state of euphoria with the Holy Spirit.

As we continued to mingle and relax, my attention was turned to a child sitting on the floor in the far corner of the room. She seemed to be crying. Moving somewhat closer to her, I noticed that everyone in the group was ignoring her. *I wondered which one of these ladies was her mother?* My eyes would not move from this young girl. Feeling a nudge on my shoulder, I looked over my shoulder; but saw no one there. *Was this my angel helper again?* The thought to go and sit by this girl increased. My mind began to argue inside of me. *Who me?* I thought. *I can't speak Spanish. What can I do to comfort this young girl?* Gradually, becoming obedient to the Holy Spirit overcame my fear and embarrassment of what others might think. My sense of being a complete stranger and foreigner diminished. The Holy Spirit came upon me in such a way that I felt compelled to go sit by the young girl on the floor. Walking over, I sat down on the floor beside her, still feeling very self-conscious. Surprisingly, no one had noticed my action or seemed to care that I was sitting by the young girl. Even the young girl had not acknowledged in any manner that I sat down beside her as she continued to cry softly.

Sitting, what seemed like ages on the floor, my mind *or something* kept telling me that this was the most foolish thing I had ever done. *You're clueless—Ferel!* I waved to the interpreter to come over and inquire what was happening with this young girl who remained motionless, continuing to cry while sitting on the floor. All of a sudden, the young girl slides over and lays her head in my lap. Thankfully, the interpreter returned in a few minutes and told me that a lady had brought this 12-year-old girl, Mia, to the meeting. She wasn't her child but belonged to a next-door neighbor.

It seemed Mia's father had died of a heart attack 15 months earlier, and she was in severe grief and depression. She told the interpreter that her father had treated her cruelly as compared to the other children in the family. This behavior caused Mia to think that her father didn't love her. However, she loved her father and wanted to ask him what she had done to make him hate her and cause his cruel behavior?" He died suddenly before she could find out and ask for his forgiveness.

Her neighbor benefactor, however, told the interpreter another story. This neighbor was in the room with Mia and her father right before he died. The neighbor heard him tell Mia how much he loved her. Mia, however, failed to hear his final declaration of love for her because she was crying so loud. To further complicate this situation, Mia couldn't understand why God took her father. Why did God dislike her? She had become more bitter, confused, and full of guilt during these past 15 months. Mia had no color in her face as she continued to sit on the floor in a fetal position with her head laying in my lap. Our interpreter remained on the floor with us. Feeling led by the Holy Spirit, I began explaining death to this young girl as a result of natural causes. I told her that I lost my first child at birth, but this was due to no fault of the mother or God. There had been natural and genetic causes of not being properly united together, which had caused my baby's stillbirth. Mia seemed to accept my reasoning at the moment. I told her, "Mia, one day God will allow you to rejoin your daddy in heaven. There, all your pain and hurt will cease. God will make right in heaven whatever went wrong here on earth. You will experience only love and joy in heaven, just as I believe that I will see my loving and beautiful child as well."

GOD WILL MAKE RIGHT IN HEAVEN WHATEVER WENT WRONG HERE ON EARTH.

The interpreter told me that she felt that the Lord wanted me to role-play with this 12-year-old girl. I would become her father; she would become my daughter. Mia could say anything to me that she desired to tell her daddy. The interpreter believed that the Spirit of the Lord would speak through this to provide the encouragement, hope, and forgiveness that she needed. Before beginning this conversation, the interpreter explained to Mia that I would sit behind her and put my arms around her. She repositioned sideways as we sat on the floor, hugging each other tightly. She placed her small arms around my neck and began to sob softly for at least 15 more minutes. Mia asked for my forgiveness concerning anything that she had done. I replied, "You have done nothing to be forgiven for. As your daddy, I am truly sorry that my attitude toward you caused you to feel that you were not loved. I love you very much."

I wiped tears from her cheeks gently and said softly, "Will you please forgive daddy for hurting you?"

"Si, si," she said as she continued to cry.

The Spirit of the Lord fell upon me in a greater way as I began to pray in the Spirit. I began to cry with her. I actually felt her pain. It broke my heart. Lovingly, I began stroking her hair while continuing to repeat that Jesus loved her very much. Continuing to cry with her, I literally felt her pain being released. I have no words that adequately describe this moment.

Minutes passed. We continued to rock back and forth on the floor as I hugged Mia. She kept on sobbing gently. Suddenly, I felt an indescribable closeness to God that I had never felt before. His presence was one of peaceful serenity with encompassing love.

As I continued to hug this sweet young girl there on the floor, my tears grew stronger and louder. I felt that the Lord was telling me that I had come to Venezuela for this young girl—for Mia. Suddenly I did not hear a voice. Instead, a typewritten message flashed across my mind that asked, "When was the last time you hugged your daughter?"

I began to cry even harder as I realized that I couldn't remember when I had hugged De'Anne last. I often told her that I loved her, but actions speak louder than words, don't they? I promised God in my mind that would be one of the first things I would do whenever I got home. I would sit on the floor with De'Anne hugging her as I had hugged Mia.

Suddenly, I felt two small hands upon my cheeks. Opening my eyes, this lovely girl was holding my face between her hands with a great big smile upon her face. Quiet singing was heard as I noticed the group had formed a circle around us. We arose from the floor to the hugs and shouts of the people praising God. Glancing at my watch, one and a half hours had passed.

Andrew told me later that this was the saddest, yet most beautiful and touching moment he had ever witnessed. He also told me how people in the group were being slain in the Spirit as this was happening. Everyone was crying as they felt the presence of God. Andrew brought me a glass of water, smiled, and hugged me as well. I couldn't help but become teary-eyed again as I continued to feel electrified by the Spirit of God. It was now close to 7:00 pm.

Unbeknownst to me, another college lad had knocked on the front door saying that the Spirit of the Lord had told him that he was needed. He obeyed. We were introduced to him. Amazing!! One interpreter would leave, and the Spirit of the Lord brought another to interpret. Our original group had gone home, but other believers had come. Singing and praying for the needs of others continued until midnight. Our hosts told us that many had never been inside this house. It was impressive how sensitive and obedient they were to the leading of the Holy Spirit.

I am still overwhelmed by this amazing outpouring of God's Spirit. This experience was remarkable! This day became like the early Christian church in action—totally dependent upon the Father, Son, and Holy Spirit. No one really wanted to end this glorious day in the Lord, but the Holy Spirit abated. Everyone was emotionally and spiritually exhausted, while I was "flying like an eagle" in the Spirit at the same time. Bethany and Ruth drove Andrew and me back to the hotel. This event would become a "benchmark of faith" for me for all eternity. I had witnessed the Bible becoming alive, as it is written, by the power of the Holy Spirit through a living Lord. GOD WAS ALIVE!! HE IS ALIVE!! God was not a figment of my imagination. Hallelujah!

I also discovered two principles that day in serving the Lord.

1. As our Lord takes imperfect people to minister to others in His name, He will also be ministering to that person's needs. Without the Spirit of the Lord, a person can do nothing.
2. Just as our Lord sent His disciples out two by two, so we go forth two by two as well. God blends the spiritual giftings of the pair together in His Spirit. No person has all His gifts.

This was our heavenly Father demonstrating His perfect love for all. That day my faith was transformed from a "religion of the mind" to a "Jesus of the heart," resulting in *Hope Beyond!*

ENDNOTE

1. Acts 10:34 TPT.

CHAPTER 7

KEEPS GETTING BETTER

*A*ndrew and I were eager to begin Sunday morning. We were still filled with excitement from the incredible time of ministry the night before. *How could it get any better than yesterday?* We had a full schedule which made us both happy, and we looked forward to the day with eager anticipation.

Around 10:00 am, we were picked up and taken to a Full Gospel Church in a very poor section of town. They were meeting in an old movie theater, where the pastor had built a speaker's platform out of rough wood. He was a young African-American minister around the age of 30. I loved his enthusiasm as he led rousing, Gospel songs with a four-piece band. Andrew smiled at me as he began to pray that the pastor would not break his foot because he was stomping it so hard as he kept in time with the music.

My previous pastoral preaching experiences helped me be comfortable in these speaking situations, especially whenever I felt led to do something different other than sharing my testimony. As Andrew finished his testimony to a lot of amens,

I felt led to leave the platform. Turning to the pastor, I said, "Tell the people that the Holy Spirit desires them to gather in a circle for prayer. Let's see what the Lord has planned for His people this morning."

Three hundred plus people in attendance eagerly jumped from their seats and joined hands together. When the commotion ceased and quiet was restored, I said, "Cleanse your hearts by uttering prayers in either Spanish or English and in your prayer language. Praise the name of Jesus!"

You could literally feel the Holy Spirit descend into that place. Some people began to shout, weep, and worship the Lord their God in freedom. All I said afterward was that our Lord wanted them to experience a "practical Jesus" who desired to answer all their needs. The pastor, Andrew, and I spent the next ninety minutes praying over children, teenagers, and adults for all types of emotional, physical, or spiritual concerns. When the session ended, I shared with the pastor, "Ask your people to share in next week's service concerning any signs, wonders, or miracles that they experienced today and during the week to come."

Why was that important? A person needs to tell what God has done for them. They may not understand it, but they cannot deny it. The faith of others increases when hearing how God is working in the lives of others.

We were taken back to the hotel. On Saturday, our previous hosts, Bethany and Ruth, took us to lunch. Afterward, they drove us to two hospitals, where we prayed for Christian believers who needed encouragement and healing from the Lord.

We were then driven to a very nice residential area for a home meeting with an upper-middle-class family who lived on the side of a mountain overlooking Caracas. We were joined by a California couple, Joe and Joanna, who would be giving their testimony. Entering the courtyard, the presence of the Holy Spirit was very strong. My skin felt "electric" as it had whenever I first read about this trip. I was beginning to realize that feelings should not lead us because feelings can mislead. This feeling, however, was one of anticipation and of knowing that the Spirit of the Lord was here to work signs and wonders. After the Californian couple and Andrew had shared their testimony, I felt led again to have the thirty or so people in attendance join hands and lead them in prayer. I sensed the Spirit causing me to focus upon certain people in the group as I was speaking. Words of knowledge came forth, filling my mind. What the Lord had begun with me the day before, He was continuing. This was all so new to me. Flowing where the Spirit was leading, my eyes fell upon a lady 20 feet away. We looked intently at one another for a brief moment. Opening my mouth, the words came forth, "You have a very compassionate heart."

Before the interpreter could repeat the entire sentence, the Holy Spirit fell upon the lady sitting there. She began sobbing heavily while dropping her shoulders. Moving towards her while praying in the Spirit, nothing else came into my mind to say. *Oh well,* I thought to myself, *have faith and trust in Him.* The lady continued crying as I laid my hand upon her shoulder, continuing to pray in the Spirit. Andrew walked up and spoke quietly in my ear that her sister, who was also in the meeting, had told him that she had specific problems with her husband, who had been abusing her. I now knew why God showed me that she had a "big heart." A compassionate heart was needed to be able to endure all that she had been going through. I asked Andrew to take over and pray with her as I returned to the front of the room.

As I turned around to face the group, another lady was already walking to the front. She asked the interpreter for me to pray for the healing of her body. These Venezuelan women are very specific about their medical problems when asking for prayer. As I began to pray, I felt led to hold her head with my hands and lay my head against her forehead. After finishing the healing prayer, I told the interpreter to say that I felt the Lord was about to give me another word for her.

"Please be patient as I pause to listen," I said.

Then, silently praying in the name of Jesus, I asked the Lord to make His word clear so I could deliver it. His word came as soon as I ended my request. I saw plainly, "the office of an intercessor." The Spirit of the Lord also told me that this lady had been called to this office previously. Intercession is a ministry for the strongest and heartiest of believers. It takes a compassionate heart, time, and great faith in praying through and assuming the burdens of others. As the interpreter relayed these words, she began to cry. Looking intently into my eyes for at least a minute, she said nothing. I continued to pray in the Spirit. It was amazing how easy it was to minister by praying in the Spirit. These people seem to hear His words like any other foreign language, especially since there were so many different Spanish dialects within Venezuela.

IT TAKES A COMPASSIONATE HEART, TIME, AND GREAT FAITH IN PRAYING THROUGH AND ASSUMING THE BURDENS OF OTHERS.

Through our interpreter, the woman told me that another minister told her the same thing in a similar house meeting five years earlier. Due to a non-believing husband and the deception of the devil, she had been robbed of this experience. She began to doubt it ever happened. She asked for God's forgiveness. Being led by the Spirit, I answered, "Can you forgive yourself? Jesus has already forgiven you. Jesus loves you so much that He sent me to you at this time as His vessel, confirming again what He gave you. Use His gift of intercession wisely and boldly. Go in His peace. Glory to God!"

Andrew returned to the front with Joe and Joanna. We continued to pray for the remaining people with any needs. Surprisingly, the Spirit of the Lord gave me instructions for Joanna as we prayed for others. I asked her, "Can you feel the Spirit flowing into the person as you prayed? Did you feel a warmth flowing from your hands into them?" This had occurred with me several times during prayers of healing, especially if they had been slain in the Spirit. How wonderful it was to share with someone as others had shared with me!

The Lord is so good! He had saved the best for last. Whenever we first entered this house, the Lord had revealed a woman sitting close to the front who was heavily burdened. I felt her pain, her guilt, and much sadness. She had a look of despair. Joanna inquired if anyone else needed prayer. I felt in my spirit that this lady needed to hear from Jesus. Suddenly the lady jumped to her feet and came forward. She began to tell Joanna how she wanted us to pray for her. I replied, "I have been waiting for you since we first began. The Lord pointed you out as we entered. He instructed me to wait until you made the first move."

Smiling and looking intently into her eyes, I asked her, "Have you been deceiving yourself? The Lord wants you to be truthful with Him about your need."

The Holy Spirit instantly fell on her. She began to cry loudly with deep sobs. I laid my hands on her shoulders while praying in the Spirit. Like a mighty blast, she was knocked to the floor being slain in the spirit. The people stood up and shouted, "Gloria a Dios! Glory to God!"

As the team rested their hands upon her, praying in the Spirit, suddenly the Lord instructed the people, "Beloved, do not be afraid. Be open to the leading of my Holy Spirit in your life. Trust in Me! I desire to give you spiritual giftings in order to bless others and use them in My service. I need everyone in this house to become a disciple for Me. Use the same methods you witnessed tonight. I will supply your every need. My mercy is healing this lady by the power of My Holy Spirit. I am your heavenly Father who knows how to give good gifts to His children."

The lady on the floor came to about one minute later. We helped her stand up; she testified that she felt completely healed of back pain, guilt, sadness, and heavy burdens. She smiled broadly. There was a glow about her face. She was in peace.

This unique experience revealed to me that I didn't have to know every detail about a person's need for the Lord to accomplish His work! The meeting was adjourned.

We had fellowship with refreshments. Hearing my name called, I turned around, and to my surprise, Bethany, who had been with us earlier, was standing there. She was motioning me to follow her outside. She told me that she had gone home to rest that afternoon but had been awakened by the Spirit of the Lord to pray for me. As we walked, I felt the Spirit jump within me. I had been told, previously, that when you get close to a very spiritual person, you might feel the presence of the Lord emanating from them. Through her broken English, Bethany explained how the Lord had instructed her to pray for my family—to pray for unity in the Spirit as one and for my ministry that she had prophesied about. The

Lord then gave her specific answers for my current situation. I lost much of her message due to her broken English and fast-talking. She was really excited as she talked. Her excitement excited me as well! These words, however, stood out; "I used your alcoholic wife to bring you back to Me, to reawaken your pastor's heart, to become more aware and compassionate for the needs and emotions of your family and others, to break through your pride for you cannot solve all things nor handle every problem."

Hearing these words brought me back to my wife's situation. I had discovered that I couldn't solve anything. The harder I tried, the more she rebelled, leading to greater frustration. A pastor once told me that an alcoholic will drink until they get sick and tired of being sick and tired.

Bethany continued, "'Therefore,' says the Lord, 'give your wife to Me. After all, you should no longer doubt after witnessing this new ministry that I am preparing you for. I am God. I Am that I Am. Never tell your wife again that she must attend church or any religious activity, for I know her, and being God, I am quite capable of handling her even as I handled you. Remember, I gave her to you in marriage!'"

Then my messenger put her finger on my chest and began to thump very hard, repeatedly saying, "You are to love! You are to love, love, **love**!"

I begin crying gently. Remembering little Mia the day before, I certainly had been convinced to show more love to my family, especially my own daughter. Looking into the eyes of this messenger, I asked her, "Does God want me to become a full-time pastor again or stay in business and minister as a lay person?"

In the short time I had known her, this lady had never failed to amaze me how she could hear from God instantly. She bowed her head, prayed in the Spirit for about 30 seconds, looked up at me, and said, "God first laughed at your question and then answered you with a question, 'You are serving me, aren't you?'"

I thanked her profusely for going out of her way to be obedient and deliver this message from the Lord. I was feeling sad since our team would be leaving Caracas soon. I might never see her again. We said our goodbyes and hugged each other. I had experienced and learned so much from God on this trip—from her and from these people. Growing to love them, I felt as if I had known them all my life. The thought occurred to me at that moment that if I hadn't had a family and business, I might have considered staying. I had experienced the unspeakable joy and the spiritual atmosphere that the Apostle Paul had written about.

As we parted, she said, "You are coming back to Venezuela."

"Yes," I replied, "I feel this in my spirit as well. Until we meet again, Bethany, may the joy, peace, and love of Jesus Christ keep you safe."

The man of the house suddenly rushed out, grabbed my hand with tears in his eyes, and said, "My house will always be your house. When you come again, you will see all my children at my side being strong believers in Christ. We will never forget you."

"I will always remember this day as well," I said. We hugged, crying unashamedly, and parted company.

As Andrew and I were getting into the vehicle, we hugged each other as well and began talking excitedly. How amazing the presence of God and the power of His Holy Spirit had been in this place! In fact, we both couldn't believe how powerful the past two days had been in the presence of God's Holy Spirit. We both noticed how loving and receptive the people had been. Every place we went reflected how spiritually hungry these people were to receive the Word of God and His power with signs, wonders, and miracles following. He acknowledged, and I agreed, how God had brought us both into new dimensions of His grace, glory, and power not experienced or encountered by either one of us previously.

Our host's teenage daughter drove us back to the hotel. It was now around 11:00 pm. We had experienced six hours of singing, prayer, and ministry. Time passes quickly whenever the glory of God comes down. As we traveled in the night, the Spirit of the Lord brought back to my memory how four months earlier, a Christian brother had come to my house.

> TIME PASSES QUICKLY WHENEVER THE GLORY OF GOD COMES DOWN.

He prayed for me to have boldness, discernment of spirits, a gift of gab, and to possess the joy of my salvation. This brother and everything that had happened since my earlier "lady in the street experience" had been preparing me for this trip to Venezuela. Everything witnessed at the deliverance services with my friend, Dustin, had manifested on this trip. I realized that all my previous pastoral experience had not been wasted.

My voice suddenly broke the silence as we rode along. "Andrew," I declared, "I believe that we have been experiencing God's perfect love! Yes, His perfect love! Think about it. Everything that we needed from the beginning of this trip until now has been perfect. Whatever we needed has been provided at just the right moment. Our ministry together has been no exception. Strangers flowing in perfect unity together by the power of His Holy Spirit as if we had done this together for many years. Every request met with signs, wonders, and miracles! Several times all

I did was just pray in the Spirit and watch what took place in the person standing before me. Just awesome, Andrew! Marvelous and stunning! Unbelievable yet undeniable! Above everything else, our heavenly Father allowed us, two ordinary guys, to participate in the outpouring of His perfect love. This was hope beyond anything that I could ever imagine or hope for! It was **Hope Beyond!**

> *"Now to him who is able to do far more abundantly than all that we ask or think, according to the power at work within us, to him be glory in the church and in Christ Jesus throughout all generations, forever and ever. Amen."*[1]

ENDNOTE

1. Ephesians 3:20-21 ESV.

CHAPTER 8

A LIGHT PIERCING THE DARKNESS

new adventure began as we set out on a bus ride from Caracas to Maracaibo. The journey of over 400 miles did not seem as long as it first appeared because of the beauty of the Venezuela landscape and because it offered a wonderful time of reflection about all that had happened in Caracas. Wow! The power of a living God through His Holy Spirit had already manifested in a way that was truly beyond all that I had desired, imagined, and hoped for. *How could it get any better?* I attempted to envision what lay before us as we minister to God's people. Time passed quickly as other small groups assembled on the bus to exchange all that they had witnessed in the places they had gone.

We arrived in mid-afternoon and were greeted at the hotel by several of our hosts. We were divided into small groups, then journeyed to private homes for an afternoon meal. The people were friendly and welcomed us with love and generous hearts. Our dwelling place had meager furnishings but was clean and adequate. As we ate the meal prepared by our host, they attended to our every need. I remember feeling that I should get up from the table and allow them to eat because it seemed like they were giving us all the food they had in their house. The atmosphere was joyful and informal, and you could feel the presence of the Lord in this place.

After the meal, one of our leaders began to minister to any needs presented to us. On one or two occasions, I believed a word came from the Spirit for me to give to persons within the house, but I stayed in the background because the prophetic word I was getting was different from the one that our leader was offering. I knew that I was still a beginner in this type of spiritual setting, and there was still much for me to learn.

We left our wonderful and gracious host. Returning to the hotel, we dressed in more formal attire, then drove to a church somewhere around Maracaibo. It was after 8:00 pm when we arrived. The darkness of night had descended. This church was unusual, however. The structure was inflatable, with huge blowers filling it with air. It could accommodate a thousand people. We were in a very poor rural setting. The people here had no access to doctors, medicine, or the basic necessities that those in our culture felt were needed for adequate living. They had no entertainment other than to go to church six days a week. As we approached the church, we heard singing and clapping as they worshiped the Lord. Entering, the place felt alive! The congregation was full of joy, anticipation, and expectation with the arrival of fellow believers from America. They seemed overwhelmed that believers from a foreign land would want to come and worship with them.

As I looked around the packed church, people were standing in every available space. There was no air-conditioning, and the ventilation system was poor. Droplets of perspiration ran down to my toes as I stood listening. Those members of the team who gave their testimonies won the hearts of the people as they spoke. The interpreters did a wonderful job in capturing the emotion of each speaker.

We joined other team members and gathered at the front of the room near the altar, following a call for further ministry. As people began to move to the front, I noticed a young mother holding a baby approaching the altar with three other women who I assumed were friends or family. She was looking around as if she was trying to decide who to go to. She came and stood in front of me. I looked around for an interpreter, but they were all busy. _What was I to do?_ Looking at the young mom and her child in front of me, I knew beyond a shadow of a doubt that her child was very sick. The child looked to be five or six months old. To be perfectly honest, I wished that she had chosen to stand in front of someone else. Green and yellow drainage from the child's nostril had accumulated for some time. It had crusted yet was glistening and wet as the drainage continued. After all, I was wearing my best suit and tie! I definitely didn't want green goo smeared on me. As I looked into the eyes of the young mother, she suddenly thrust her child into my arms while clasping her hands together in a prayer posture.

My insides were churning, and being anxious is a mild description. _What was I to do?_ So, I said, "Okay, Lord, you got me into this mess. Help!"

Immediately I saw the word, "Pray!" Not knowing what to pray, I began praying in my prayer language. Within 30 seconds, I began to feel an unusual warm sensation in both feet. They were tingling like my feet were falling asleep but also being overtaken by an unmistakable warmth that I had never experienced before. This warm feeling grew intensely! It began to flow upward until I felt immersed, as if I was in very warm water. To my surprise, as this feeling of warmth reached my shoulders, I felt it flowing into my fingers. From my fingers, the warm sensation flowed into the child. As this was happening, I drew the child close to me. Its small face touched my cheek. The child was very hot with a fever. I no longer cared whether that child was smearing its green mucus on my suit. Love and compassion had overcome me! Continuing to pray in the Spirit, I hugged the child tightly in my arms. I lost track of time and was engrossed in the moment. Suddenly the small child moved. Turning its face, I could feel the cheek on the other side. It was cold! It was as cold as it had been hot just a few moments ago!

I whispered, "Thank you, Lord!"

I felt tears moving downward from my eye as I gave the small child back to the mother. As soon as she placed the child's forehead on her cheek, she discovered what I already knew. There was no fever! God had healed her child! She immediately began talking to her three friends. Together they began jumping up and down shouting. "Gloria a Dios! Glory to God!"

Overcome with the emotion of what had taken place, I also raised my hands, shouting, "Glory to God! Praise the Lord! Glory to God! Thank you, Lord, for your healing mercy!"

The celebration lasted at least five minutes. Afterward, the young mom and her friends hugged me, saying, "Gracias señor, gracias. Gloria a Dios!"

Continuing in the afterglow of what had happened, I knew God's light had pierced the darkness of doubt and pride in the heart of this imperfect vessel. His light had penetrated the despair of a young mother's heart, restoring faith, hope, and love. *"Now faith is the assurance of things hoped for, the conviction of things not seen."*[1]

The hour was late when we arrived at the hotel. Most of us slept until almost lunchtime the next day, cherishing a day of rest, relaxation, and opportunities to take pictures. We shopped at the local merchants as we toured a native Indian village, Sinamaica, and then assembled back together later that afternoon. Two of our team members, who stayed behind, told the group of an unusual event. One of them had noticed that a dog had fallen into a manhole opening about six feet under the sidewalk and could not get out. Just then, two teenage boys happened by and agreed to help rescue this dog. Following the rescue, they invited the boys for refreshments at the hotel. They witnessed to the boys and led them in a prayer of salvation to Jesus Christ as their Lord and Savior. Then they prayed for the boys to receive the baptism of the Holy Spirit as evidenced by speaking in their own prayer language. They received! Hallelujah! Two team members rescued a dog and two teenagers!

Just a coincidence? Don't think so! Once again, it was the perfect love of God orchestrating time, people, and events to bring about His will and purpose so that the individual will be able to partner with Him in bringing about His Kingdom on earth. Amazing! Incredible! Incomprehensible! Yet it happens right in front of your

GOD ORCHESTRATES TIME, PEOPLE, AND EVENTS TO BRING ABOUT HIS WILL AND PURPOSE.

eyes! Undeniable! God's light piercing the darkness! Truly, **Hope Beyond!**

The team was looking forward with expectation and anticipation for the banquet given for believers and non-believers the next night after hearing about this experience and encounter. What would God do next?

The next day seven of us gathered at the hotel swimming pool around midafternoon while waiting for the banquet that would begin later that night. What a wonderful time of fellowship with fellow believers as we confessed our weaknesses and needs to one another. We prayed for each other. My prayer request focused upon my need for greater love, compassion, and unity within my family. Concluding the prayers for me, a sister in the Lord took my hand, looked intently into my eyes and said, "Faithful is He that calls you, and faithful is He who will also do it!"

As people came for the banquet that night, our team leader requested that we separate and sit at different tables. Walking into the banquet room, I noticed most of the tables were full; however, one table before me had one seat left. I walked towards it and decided to sit there. A teenage boy sat next to me. Thankfully, he could speak some English. His name was Jesse.

Asking me where I lived in America, I replied, "Texas."

With that, he laughed and said, "You're not tall enough to be a Texan. I thought all Texans look like cowboys wearing chaps and spurs."

"Where did you get that idea?" I asked.

He replied, "Everything I know about Texas is from watching John Wayne movies. He's my favorite cowboy!"

Following his reply, I heard the Lord whisper in my ear, "Give him your Texas belt buckle."

For those of you who know me and for those of you who don't, I confess that I have a sense of pride about my possessions and do not give them up easily. During this season of my life, I thought of them more highly than I ought to.

In my mind, I thought, *Lord, is this really you? If this is an evil spirit, put it behind me?* Instantly I saw in my mind's eye the phrase, "Give him your belt buckle!"

"Okay, Lord," I said, "I will!"

Pushing my chair back, I briefly stood, taking off my belt. Sitting back down, I unfastened the buckle from the belt. It was outlined in gold trim with a silver finish. It was a special rendition of the fiftieth anniversary of the Texas Farm Bureau. I knew that the people at my table were watching me do this, but I was unaware that the Holy Spirit had gotten the attention of everyone at the head table. They were also watching. This young man could not contain his emotion. He jumped up and hugged me with great enthusiasm. He was overwhelmed and touched by my gesture of generosity.

A Venezuelan general and Victor, our team's retired general, were sitting together with their wives and other dignitaries at the head table. Our general's wife, Candace, came to me when the banquet was over and shared how the atmosphere at the head table had been awkward and stuffy before they saw what was taking place between the teenager and me. She explained how the Holy Spirit had directed her to witness what was taking place at my table. Then she directed those at the head table to watch also. As the head table observed this act of love and generosity between two strangers, the atmosphere changed from stiffness and coldness to warmth and friendliness.

This event helped the non-believing general and his wife open their minds and hearts to receive the testimony they were about to hear. She continued to tell me how amazing the Spirit of the Lord was in directing a Texan to sit next to a teenager who was thrilled with the cowboy legend, John Wayne. It's astounding how God could use a simple act of giving to break the ice among a group of believers and non-believers. At the invitation for anyone to accept Christ as their Lord and Savior, this high-ranking, Venezuelan general and wife raised their hands. The next day the Venezuelan general invited Victor and Candace to their home, where their entire family and staff received Jesus Christ as their Lord and Savior. They were all baptized. God's light continued to pierce the darkness!

As I left this young man at the banquet's close, I invited him and his Christian dad to be my guest at breakfast in the morning with my roommate, Andrew. We arose with anticipation and I wondered, *Would the young teenager and his dad be there to join us for breakfast?* Going down to breakfast, the father and son were there awaiting our arrival. They both gave us hugs and greetings. The young lad proudly pointed to his wearing the belt buckle. He told me, "I will always treasure this gift from the tiny Texan with a big heart. I will proudly pass it on to my future sons. It will be a treasure within our family for as long as I live."

Over breakfast, we discussed forming a men's Christian fellowship. Later that morning, the Spirit of the Lord prompted us to pray for this young man to receive the baptism of the Holy Spirit with evidence of receiving his prayer language. This was the first time that I participated in praying and witnessing what was happening between Andrew and this young man. Praise the Lord! I will never forget the moment when the Spirit of the Lord fell upon him. So intent was this young man that he perspired greatly as he prayed for some time in the Spirit. Finally, I felt led to hug him and instructed him to relax.

He inquired of us, "What happened?"

Andrew began a teaching session with him to better understand and confirm his encounter, which also furthered my understanding. As the meeting ended, his dad handed me a gift of cheese, continuing to thank me profusely for my generosity. His gift of delicious goat's milk cheese accompanied me to Texas along with the story. I enjoyed telling how two families had come to know the saving grace and love of our Lord through the gift of a belt buckle to a teenager from a tiny Texan with a big heart!

Our team leader accepted the invitation of the interpreter who had been with us in Maracaibo, to his mother's house. She lived on a small farm outside the city. He was so proud to tell us that his mother had been a Christian believer for 64 years. Their home was a small, neat house surrounded by a small picket fence and adorned with pictures of the family and their native land. The soil was so rocky that it was difficult to understand how the land produced anything. They were fortunate to have water in a spring-fed creek that flowed throughout their property. The land was fertile, however, as evidenced by the avocados, coconuts, papayas, oranges, mangoes, and an assortment of vegetables they grew. They also had chickens for fresh eggs and meat, cows for milk and butter, and hogs for pork. It was a self-sustaining farm that took everyone's efforts daily. A wonderful lunch was placed before us that was produced by this farm entirely. It was a delicious meal of chicken soup, fresh green salad mixed with tomatoes, peppers, cucumbers, pickles, and onions. The main dish was *hallaca*—a food that had a cornmeal texture similar to a tamale but much bigger. It was filled with bits of chicken, pork, beef, onions, olives, and other things baked in banana leaves. It was pleasing to the taste and very satisfying.

Returning, we arrived at the hotel around 4:00 pm. Our team leader announced that we had been invited to attend a house church in downtown Maracaibo before the evening banquet. He wondered if the four men who did not have their wives with them on this trip would attend this service. All the other team members and wives would begin preparation for the banquet that evening. We four were more than happy to fulfill his request. The bus dropped us at the house church as the others went back to the hotel.

The church building was long and spacious. I estimated that it could seat 300 people easily. Seventy-five worshipers were singing and clapping, mostly women of all ages. The leader of the praise band motioned for us to sit at the front. We were invited to give our testimonies. As my turn came, I felt led by the Spirit to invite everyone to begin praying. I felt that signs and wonders would be manifested in our presence, especially all types of healing. After several minutes of praying, our team leader stood up, explaining that before we enter into the service of healing, any doubter in the Lord's ability to heal—those who did not have an open mind to receive by faith such an experience—needed to leave. I remembered what I believed to be a spiritual law found in the book of Romans, where it talks about God who gives life to the dead and calls things that are not as though they were.[2] And as he continued to speak, another Scripture came to my mind when Jesus said, *"Let the little children come to me and do not hinder them, for to such belongs the kingdom of heaven."*[3]

Suddenly our attention was drawn to a door on the left front side where we were sitting. We noticed an older lady talking loudly in Spanish while pointing to those of us sitting on the front row. She was surrounded by approximately six or seven other women who were listening to her. This group began to move towards the worship leader, who was also our interpreter. They engaged in conversation with him for several minutes. He turned to us and related that this woman and her 14-year-old granddaughter had walked from a village approximately 20 miles from the city. She had taken this journey because of a vision. In the vision, she saw four gringos gathered in the city that would heal her demon-possessed granddaughter. Her granddaughter had sporadic, hysterical ravings and fits in her village since the age of five. The older lady had become very excited and was pointing at us four team members because she had seen our faces in her vision. Marveling at what I was hearing, it was truly unbelievable how this grandmother and her granddaughter walked 20 miles into a city of over a million people. There, she was led to a house church where she had never gone before and found four gringos!

The worship leader placed a chair in front of the podium and motioned the young girl to sit down. He called our leader to the front. They were having a conversation, I assume, about what to do. The young girl sat with no expression and no movement of any kind. I sensed an urging to go sit by this girl, similar to what I had felt at the first house church experience in Caracas. Standing up, I took my chair and placed it beside her. Sitting down, she did not make any movement or acknowledgment of any kind that I, a stranger, had sat down beside her. For some reason, I placed my hand in her hand. Still no movement from the girl, but she allowed me to hold her hand. Hearing the conversation continuing behind me, I heard our team leader ask the question, "How do we know she is demon-possessed?"

Someone answered, "If a demon-possessed person hears the name of Jesus, they will respond."

As I heard the word, Jesus, this girl suddenly became alive! She straightened up in her chair. Immediately, her hands became like panther claws, literally trying to tear my eyes out! It was taking all my strength to keep this from happening! I was in fairly decent shape from my occupation and from taking care of my small livestock farm; however, this girl's strength was amazing! I couldn't help but notice that this young girl's eyes had become as black as a panther. Her right eye had a dancing red dot in it. In the meantime, my three other teammates and the interpreter were helping to subdue this 14-year-old girl. We got her to the floor on her back. Two other women came to assist us. I held one leg by the ankle while the other teammates held her other leg, arms, and hands. One of the women laid across her waist while the other lady laid across her chest. The interpreter was just above her head. My mind raced back to witnessing demonic activity while attending the services of my deliverance friend. I now wished I had listened and watched better on how Dustin ministered to others in this condition. I was not prepared for this situation. Continuing to breathe heavily and excitedly, I held her leg—her strength was amazing! It was taking all six of us to keep her on the floor. The only Scripture that I could think of to declare was, "*I can do all things through Christ who strengthens me.*[4] Be delivered in Jesus' name."

I kept shouting this continuously as I held on. Looking in the direction of the young girl's face, I noticed her eyes. Still black, they had also become covered with a white glaze that looked very similar to the glaze that a person sees on a doughnut. She was also frothing at the mouth like a rabid dog. I could not believe such an experience was happening. It was real and occurring right before my eyes! Even then, it was incredible and inconceivable. I continued to join my teammates, the interpreter, and the women in praying in the Spirit. We declared Scripture phrases over her. She continued fighting us with all her strength. This went on for approximately 20 minutes when the young girl suddenly ceased all movement and seemed to relax her body. As she appeared to be relaxing, everyone began to feel the warmth of God's healing power. Everyone, however, continued to hold on.

Andrew asked the team leader, "Has she been delivered?"

The interpreter kept talking to the girl without response, and one of the women stated, "Her hands have relaxed, and the glaze has disappeared from her eyes."

Looking at her eyes, however, I noticed that they were still black. It seemed that five or more minutes had passed when suddenly the girl began again. I guess that she must have been pausing for her second wind. Holy anger began to arise within my spirit. It was disappointing that it appeared all of our efforts had been wasted. *Was God trying to instruct us in this matter?* Everyone began to shout and declare Scriptures again. In the midst of this, I suddenly saw a phrase in my mind, "Ask Me."

"Ask you what, Lord?" I thought.

He replied, "Ask Me what spirits need to be cast out from this girl."

"Okay," I prayed, "What spirits should we cast out?"

His answer came immediately, "Cast out the spirits of ridicule, fear, and rejection!"

"Thank you, Lord!" I breathed. Then, I got the interpreter's attention and told him what I had heard in the Spirit. He began to declare that word over the young girl. Within three minutes, she was calm once again. The team continued to declare God's Word over the girl. In a few minutes, I noticed her eyes were no

HE TURNED TO THE GROUP WITH A BIG SMILE ON HIS FACE AND ANNOUNCED THAT GOD HAD DELIVERED HER!

longer black. The interpreter kept talking. Suddenly the girl began to respond to his words. They carried on a conversation for ten minutes at least. Based on her responses, he turned to the group with a big smile on his face and announced that God had delivered her! We all relaxed as the interpreter and the two women helped her to stand up. As they stood together, Andrew remarked to the interpreter, "Reassure the girl that God loves her very much and not to be fearful of our group. Tell her that her grandmother is also here."

After reassuring her, the two women took her to rejoin her grandmother and continued praying and talking with this young girl. The interpreter informed us that if we were patient, this young girl would reappear to tell her testimony of what had happened. As I was waiting for her to reappear, my mind reflected upon all that had taken place. *Wow!* The Lord certainly wanted me to experience this event in leading me to take her hand. What I had witnessed was incredible. Participating in this deliverance made an indelible impression that would last for a lifetime! I can still see her hands becoming like claws trying to gouge my eyes. I can still see that dancing red dot in her eye that was a manifestation of demonic spirits inside of her. I can still feel that superhuman strength that she demonstrated.

The young 14-year-old interrupted my thoughts as she reappeared and began sharing her testimony. She started by trying to tell what she felt. When the love of Jesus moved into her heart, body, and spirit, she felt a heavy weight being lifted from her as she lay on her back. She then relayed how she could remember having hysterical fits and running throughout her village whenever the demon manifested. She was conscious of it happening and wanted it to stop, but she had no control over it. Other than that, she could not describe when she returned to normalcy; however, she was now smiling and looking like a beautiful innocent teenager. Her eyes were actually brown, not black. She ended her testimony by thanking us, four gringos, who brought her from death to life in Jesus. She left the podium and walked over to give each of us a great big hug! She certainly had become a new creature in Christ Jesus right before our eyes! Amazing! Unbelievable yet undeniable! It was real and happened in front of nearly 100 witnesses. Hallelujah! Praise the Lord! Jesus is alive! The Holy Spirit is powerful in the name of Jesus!

We serve a living God that is not a figment or fantasy of our imagination. For us to try to understand and comprehend how God can orchestrate time, people, and events to bring about His will on earth for the love of His people is incomprehensible. He brought the four of us from America, gave a vision to a grandmother in Venezuela who saw our faces, and directed her footsteps to a city with over one million people where she had never traveled before. The grandmother believed and was obedient, resulting in her granddaughter being healed. I believe the teenager left the city normal in every way, never to forget the unfathomable love of God for her.

The banquet at the hotel that night was anti-climactic for me. What a sensational ending God revealed as He manifested His perfect love in delivering and healing this young girl.

I desire that sharing these experiences will help believers and non-believers alike grow either in their relationship with our Lord or discover a loving God for the first time in their lives. God's love is real. GOD IS ALIVE! God's love sent both the lady in the street and a deliverance minister just to me. He later called me to a foreign land over 2,000 miles from my home to discover HIS REALITY! This "doubting Thomas" would no longer doubt. I would believe in God and His Word as written in the Holy Bible forevermore. *"In Him was life [and the power to bestow life], and the life was the Light of men. The Light shines on in the darkness, and the darkness did not understand it or overpower it or appropriate it or absorb it [and is unreceptive to it]."*[5]

These mission field experiences would become benchmarks for my faith that would withstand all the fiery darts of the evil one. Yes, God's light pierces the darkness. His light is greater than the darkness! God brings forth hope! Yes, a hope that God cares for you. A hope that God will walk with you if given the chance. God will take you by His Hand and lead you through every valley. God will address every need that you have. God will cry with you when you get frustrated. He will rejoice with you when you're happy! God's perfect love ushers forth your **Hope Beyond!**

ENDNOTES

1. Hebrews 11:1 ESV.
2. Romans 4:17 KJV (paraphrased).
3. Matthew 19:14 ESV.
4. Philippians 4:13 NKJV.
5. John 1:4-5 AMP.

CHAPTER 9

ßECOME ℓIKE A ßUTTERFLY

en days after our arrival, at 7:30 am, we departed for home. Looking out the plane window, I looked fondly at the country that Christopher Columbus had nicknamed "The Land of Grace." Our mission team had certainly experienced God's grace in so many marvelous and remarkable ways. It had truly been an unforgettable experience. Now, reality was beginning to set in. Where the team had been grouped together on our flights to Venezuela, everyone was now separated except for the husbands and wives. I relaxed in my seat and was thankful that no one was sitting next to me. My thoughts turned to Andrew, my roommate, who had been such a delightful Christian brother and a partner in ministry. He had been a helpful and patient teacher in explaining the various methods of ministry that we encountered. We had worked in love, patience, and unison together with grace given by our Lord and the Holy Spirit. Unforgettable moments had been witnessed. Often, we would just sit back and allow the Holy Spirit to do His work. I marveled at how much I had learned in so short a time.

The real challenge now lay before me, though I knew that I could never forget the manifestations of the signs, wonders, and miracles I had witnessed. The benchmark of my rediscovered faith had been established. Old habits, schedules, and new spiritual understanding are not easily changed. Family and friends cannot fully appreciate my different spiritual perspective since they have not witnessed what I have seen. The demands of my business and family will now take precedent, even though I might desire isolation for continued spiritual growth. Yes, transformation is more easily said than attained. A greater understanding of the words of the Apostle Paul comes to mind; *"I do not understand what I do. For what I want to do, I do not do, but what I hate I do."*[1]

From the words received from God through my Venezuelan brothers and sisters, I knew I had to act on them and face the many challenges ahead—demonstrating greater love to family, restructuring how I spent my time, continuing to prepare for whatever the Lord might require, learn from this experience, and above all, trust God in obedience. The task would not be easy; however, I now possessed something I did not have before.

I had discovered the heart of God. I had discovered a Jesus in my heart instead of merely possessing a religion of the mind. I was "fully convinced that God was able to do what he had promised."[2]

The constant sound of the airplane's engines was lulling me to sleep. Beginning to unwind, I suddenly realized what an emotional and spiritual high I had been on for the last ten days. A sense of exhaustion was rising inside of me. Suddenly, waking to a light tap on my shoulder, my eyes opened to see the general's wife standing above me. Candace asked, "Do you mind if I sit down and visit with you for a moment?"

"Of course not," I replied, "I am humbled and honored that you would spend time with me."

This Christian lady reflected poise, grace, friendliness, and loving mannerisms in so many ways that every person meeting her for the first time would feel as though they had known her forever. Having heard my brief testimony and witnessing how the Spirit of the Lord had worked through Andrew and me, she began the conversation by confirming God's love for me in a unique and special manner. Then she related how this trip represented a new beginning and a new season that I was entering into.

"Do you know the story of how a butterfly is created?" Candace inquired.

"No," I replied, "but I would love to hear it!"

Candace began, "Let me start by saying that I felt in my spirit for several days that the Lord wanted me to share this story with you. From my own experience, I know that you are entering into a new spiritual journey and season for your life. This trip placed you on the mountain top with our Lord. Now, you will be able to descend into the valley and walk through it with His help. Your spiritual growth may be slow, arduous, and challenging. What you have witnessed will help develop your faith and provide the tools you need to grow in intimacy with the Lord. Stay balanced throughout the journey. Allow the Lord to guide every step you take."

She went on to share with me that the story of how a caterpillar turns into a butterfly is a simple parallel to a person's spiritual journey. "At just the correct time," she said, "the caterpillar will attach itself to a small branch and spin a cocoon about itself for protection. While in that cocoon, everything changes. All that the caterpillar was is dissolved and gets rearranged. Then based upon the species, it may take several weeks or longer for the transformation process to be complete and for that caterpillar to change into a butterfly."

She continued, "Interpretation of the steps may vary, but as I see it, we must firmly attach ourselves to the Word of God. As the caterpillar feeds itself within the cocoon, it continues through the process of turning into a butterfly. Likewise, we feed on His Word. Our prayers provide truth, revelation, and knowledge during our transformation process of becoming a new creature in Christ Jesus. All the old, familiar things pass away as we step into our true identity and embrace the beauty of our purpose.

"The caterpillar appears lifeless in its cocoon, but amazing activity is taking place within. As butterfly wings are being formed, a small hole opens at the bottom of the cocoon. There the butterfly begins attempting to push itself through the hole. It continues to mature through the struggles of trying to be free. If someone disturbs the cocoon or tries to speed up the process and open the cocoon for the butterfly, it will die. It needs the struggle in order to become strong. Struggle is part of the process.

"You must realize that patience is needed in your spiritual journey. You may also struggle and feel life's challenging pressure during this process of spiritual growth and intimacy. You may cry out for rescue or want to escape the struggle, but God's hand never leaves you.[3] He will take you through at your own pace. He gave you free will and the power to choose.[4] He does not force you to do anything that you do not want to do. He sees your end from the beginning,[5] and He is at work.[6] Even when you may feel like He has paused or forgotten you, He is there."[7]

She smiled and shared a Scripture with me. *"Consider it pure joy, my brothers and sisters, whenever you face trials of many kinds, because you know that the testing of your faith produces perseverance. Let perseverance finish its work so that you may be mature and complete, not lacking anything."*[8]

Candace continued, "We witness the wonder and beauty that a butterfly attains in flight. Likewise, Ferel, others will witness your spiritual growth as you mature in the giftings that He has blessed you with. How amazing is the love that God demonstrates to those who earnestly seek Him! He takes the 'ordinary' person and transforms them into the 'extraordinary' person."

She offered a prayer over me, then gave me one closing Scripture before departing back to her seat. "Ferel," she said, "the Apostle Paul discovered this important truth during his journey to spiritual maturity and greater intimacy with our Lord. Paul said, *'Three times I pleaded with the Lord to relieve me of this. But he answered me, "My grace is always more than enough for you, and my power finds its full expression through your weakness."*

'So, I will celebrate my weaknesses, for when I'm weak I sense more deeply the mighty power of Christ living in me. So, I'm not defeated by my weakness, but delighted! For when I feel my weakness and endure mistreatment—when I'm surrounded with troubles on every side and face persecution because of my love for Christ—I am made yet stronger. For my weakness becomes a portal to God's power.'9 Do you see, Ferel? God is with you in whatever lies ahead!"

I grabbed her hand as she stood up in the plane's aisle and said, "Thank you so much! I will treasure the butterfly story, and your wisdom shared with me in this moment forever. Thank you. Thank you. May the Lord continue to bless and lift up His countenance upon you, Victor, and your loved ones. Amen."

I looked out the airplane window and pondered all that Candace said to me. She had discovered through her journey that God usually reveals His truth and knowledge to a person gradually, over time. God does not view time as we do, but He will lead us as we grow in our personal relationship with Him. He desires to hear our voice, just as much as we desire to hear His voice. This relationship matures through prayer and the reading of His Word. There will come a time when you emerge from this process. Your feelings of spiritual success may cause you to step out prematurely and attempt service for Him, believing that you can accomplish anything. Please remember that as the butterfly completely emerges from its cocoon, its wings are still wet. The wings must be dry before the butterfly can take flight. Faith and obedience are not how you might feel at that moment. Stay balanced and be honest with yourself. You may not be quite ready to soar with Him as an eagle in full flight; because, like the butterfly, your wings may not be mature enough yet to engage in full flight overcoming the ups and downs that you will encounter. As a pilot of an airplane has a checklist prior to takeoff, I encourage you to do a checklist with yourself and God before your takeoff into the service of our Lord. We cannot do anything on our own or in our own strength—we must remain in Him.

"Jesus said, 'I am the vine; you are the branches.
If you remain in me and I in you, you will bear much fruit;
apart from me you can do nothing.'" [10]

It was an extraordinary spiritual story and illustration of *Hope Beyond* for my new season!

ENDNOTES

1. Romans 7:15.
2. Romans 4:21 ESV.
3. Psalm 139:7-10.
4. Genesis 2:16-17.
5. Isaiah 46:9-11.
6. Romans 8:28.
7. Hebrews 13:5.
8. James 1:2-4.
9. 2 Corinthians 12:8-10 TPT. Note: *The Passion Translation* was not yet available at the time of my conversation with the general's wife. I love the way this translation shares this important truth she shared with me.
10. John 15:5 (emphasis added).

CHAPTER 10

BACK TO REALITY

The remaining flight back to Miami and then another to Houston were without incident. I arrived home around midnight and found everyone fast asleep. Receiving and giving hugs all around the next morning, I could hardly wait until we would meet around the supper table so I could begin telling them about the trip.

Back at the office, as I greeted and received greetings from my employees, I thought to myself, *how long will the afterglow from the trip last?* Within an hour, the glow lifted as I heard all about the problems that had occurred in my absence. I'm not sure if anything went right while I was gone—vehicles broke down, competitors took three of my better accounts, and one of our convenience stores had a theft. *Was it an attack by Satan?* I'm still not sure, but one thing I know for certain, reality was staring me in the face! That night, I shared with Nita how grateful I was that she did not tell me about what was going on in my absence; otherwise, I would have possibly lost focus in serving the Lord and receiving all that He had for me to discover in Venezuela.

My children filled their plates and headed to watch their favorite television program. I asked them if we could sit at the table together. I had a few things to share with them from the trip. It was a pleasant surprise to see them sit at the table without the usual remark, "Oh, dad, do we have to?" I wanted to keep the promises I had made to God while in Venezuela; I was unsure how to try relating, loving, and unifying the family; since I had previously done such a poor job. My first words to them were really a confession that was difficult and embarrassing but it was where I thought best to begin. "I have not been a very good father or husband," I began. Confessing this to them was emotionally distressing to me. I looked into the eyes of Wes and De'Anne and told them that I had wanted to raise them in an atmosphere of outward expressions of love. Then I looked into the eyes of my wife, and I pledged to be more expressive in my love for her, too.

"This is no excuse," I shared, "my parents loved me a great deal, but they were never outwardly expressive with their love, so I just never really learned how."

Nita said, "He's telling the truth, kids," then went on to share how she was just the opposite in showing love. Her parents had always been very expressive in showing love through hugs, words, and kisses. In fact, the first time she met my parents, she walked right up to them and gave them a big hug. They were taken aback by this gesture.

"That's true," I nodded. "You took them way off guard! None of us were openly affectionate, and we weren't quite sure how to take someone who was."

I smiled at the memory and then told the kids, "It was your mother who was totally responsible for getting me and other members of my family to express our emotions outwardly. I sincerely wanted to raise you more like your mother had been—hugs, kisses, cuddles. Honestly, that was my desire, but I guess I didn't realize how much the way I grew up affected my behavior towards all of you. I'm sorry."

The room was quiet, everyone paying careful attention. After a moment, I continued, "My parents were loving to both my brother and me. We knew they loved us, but they had been raised in the generation that experienced two world wars and the harsh Depression. Times were hard. Money was scarce. I know you guys have heard me tell the story again and again about how my dad ate nothing but cornbread and milk for six weeks. That was all they had to eat. I know I heard the story about a thousand times! I'm not trying to lessen my responsibility or offer excuses for my failures in telling you these things. I have been preoccupied with business survival. East Texas has too few customers and far too many competitors, but that is no excuse. My family," I sighed deeply, "is more important to me than the business!"

Tears welled up, and I fought to keep my emotions at bay. "Please," I looked each of them in the eyes, "please have patience with me. I realize that old habits will be hard to break. I will try to become the best dad and husband I can be. You each deserve the best from me."

De'Anne spoke first and said, "That's okay, Dad. Don't be so hard on yourself."

Wes laughed and said, "If you forget your promise, Dad, I'll remind you. You can clean my fish aquarium to help you remember the next time."

Nita's eyes flashed as she piped in, "Hey! That reminds me, son. I believe I've been asking you to clean your fish aquarium for at least a couple of weeks. Why not give your fish a break? Give them some clean water this weekend?"

"Okay, Mom," he shrugged, smiling, "I knew I shouldn't have brought the aquarium up the moment I said it!"

Laughter broke the tension and relaxed everyone—especially me. Sharing like this was good for all. It united us as a family. Sadly, I couldn't remember when we had talked like this together. For the rest of the meal, they asked questions about the trip. It was fun sharing the details, remembering, and giving them the gifts that I had purchased.

As the children left the table to complete their homework, I joined my wife in helping her clear the table. As I washed the dishes, I briefly related to her the experience at the first house gathering with Mia, the 12-year-old girl. Telling this event to my daughter was a promise that I made to do upon my return. Putting the drying towel down, Nita gave me a hug from the back and said, "That would be a wonderful expression of love to your daughter."

Turning around, wet hands and all, we embraced as tears flowed.

Having finished cleaning the kitchen, I walked down the hall to my daughter's bedroom to see if she had finished her homework.

"All done?" I asked.

De'Anne was sitting on the bed reading a book and replied, "Yes, all finished!"

"Would you join me in the living room?" I asked. "I have a story to tell you about one of my experiences in Venezuela."

"Sure, Dad, I'll join you in about 5 minutes," she answered.

"That's great," I replied, walking back to the living room.

Sitting down on the floor, I began to pray silently that the Holy Spirit would join us in our conversation and help me remember every detail that happened.

De'Anne walked into the living room and was surprised to see me sitting on the floor. "What's up?" she inquired.

"If you don't mind," I replied, patting the floor with my hand, "I want to share with you an experience that I had with Mia, a 12-year-old girl from Venezuala, just like it happened."

"Okay," she said and sat down next to me.

"We had taken our first break at this house church," I began, "when I noticed this preteen girl sitting on the floor in the far corner of the room, sobbing quietly. Looking around the room, I wondered where her mother was and why had no one noticed her. She was being completely ignored. A few minutes later, I felt compelled to go sit by her on the floor. After sitting there a few minutes, the young girl moved closer and placed her head on my lap. She continued crying, so I placed my arms around her. I felt pretty embarrassed, and I kept looking around the room to see if anyone was watching, but everyone continued to ignore us. I waved to my interpreter to join me. When Kemena sat down next to us, I asked her to inquire who this sobbing child belonged to. I waited while Kemena tapped on people's shoulders and asked about the young girl. She was gone about five minutes. When she returned, Kamena sat behind me and said, 'It seems this girl's father died six months ago, and she has been in severe depression ever since. She is convinced that her father didn't love her. He died before she could ask him why his behavior was cruel in ignoring her?"

De'Anne leaned against me. Placing my arm around her, I continued, "Mia's mother was not present. A neighbor who had been trying to console the girl brought her to the meeting.

Kemena said, 'The girl's mother, this neighbor, and Mia had all been in the room when her father spoke, telling her that he loved her very much just before he died. Both the mother and the neighbor tried to tell her what the father said, but Mia failed to hear him because of her incessant crying and grief.'"

"Poor thing," De'Anne said.

"It was sad," I agreed. "Feeling led by the Holy Spirit, Kemena suggested that I role-play as the girl's father and let her ask me any questions she wanted to ask."

My daughter raised her eyebrows and looked at me quizzically.

"I know," I shook my head, "It doesn't sound like me. I still don't fully comprehend how this all happened, but the loving Holy Spirit allowed our conversation to last about 30 to 40 minutes. Mia asked me heartfelt questions about her father's behavior and why he didn't love her. As best I knew how, with the help of the Holy Spirit, I role-played as her dad, expressing my love for her. I asked her to forgive me for my failure to be the dad she needed. Finally, this sweet young girl received her healing assurance from the Lord. She knew her daddy loved her! It was amazing! I sat there all that time with my arms around her, and we cried together. Every question she asked me, I answered with the help of the Holy Spirit, whom I believe provided me with every answer."

De'Anne and I sat together, taking in the moment. Then I looked directly into my daughter's eyes and said, "As my conversation was ending with Mia, suddenly I saw a question in my mind that read, 'How long has it been since you hugged your daughter?'"

Heartfelt emotion welled up, and tears engulfed me again as the Holy Spirit fell, just as He did in Venezuela. I drew De'Anne close to me while placing both arms around her in a big bear hug.

Reciprocal tears flowed from my daughter as we continued to sit and soak up the moment.

"Please forgive me," I whispered. "I love you very, very much. You have been a bundle of love and joy, both to me and your mom. You are as beautiful inside as you are outside. I'm prejudiced. You are the best daughter any father could have! I'm proud of all that you have accomplished!"

Turning to face me, she said, "I need to make an honest confession also, dad. This talk means so much to me because …" her voice broke, "… because I wasn't sure that you loved me. There have even been times when I was unsure that I could even approach you."

I cried fresh tears as she expressed her pain—my failure as a dad. Remembering back, I suddenly realized that she had been too young to remember a dad who fed her the bottle many times during the wee hours of the morning, so her mom could get some rest. She was too little to remember how I delighted in holding her and bouncing her on my knees. She couldn't remember a dad who heard her cries in the night, who tried responding to her every need.

Yes, Lord, I thought to myself, *Your point is well received! Affection and love are to be expressed all the time!*

She squeezed me tightly, and her bear hug brought me back to the moment. "Thank you, dad," she said, "I really needed that! I love you very much."

"Thank you, my loving and forgiving daughter, for allowing me to share this experience with you. Better get to bed now. It's late. Love you! Good night." I kissed her on top of her head and sent her off to her room.

I sat and reflected on our conversation. It had been emotionally draining but revealing. My resolve to be a better father was deepened. *How could I forget something so obvious? Why should my children remember my loving actions when they were babies?*

Loving God and loving our neighbor with all of our heart, mind, soul, and strength is continuous![1] How could I ever forget that admonition?

"Forgive me, Lord, for failing to love as I have been loved. Thank you, Lord, for ministering to me as You have ministered to others."

It is still unfathomable to me how this unseen God orchestrates time, people, and events to demonstrate His love for us undeserving rascals. Wow! How He manifested His love to the many lives in Venezuela. His love was so incredible, and it was demonstrated repeatedly! Why? Why does this one God, our heavenly Father, create and desire us to be in loving relationship with Him? It is too great a mystery to comprehend!

"Live life to the fullest," God declares, "by joining with Him in being transformed into His Glory." Let us love the One who first loved us! Let us partner with Him in bringing His kingdom on earth—not only for our own life but also for the lives of others. This awe-inspiring demonstration of an all-sufficient, loving God will allow us to discover His heart, providing us with the foundation for our faith, assurance, and love that leads to **Hope Beyond.**

ENDNOTE

1. Matthew 22:36-40.

CHAPTER 11

God's Grand Design

I wish I could say that life got easier over the next sixty days or that my "spiritual afterglow" continued. It didn't. Our best-laid plans and hopes often go awry whenever we come face-to-face with the demands of everyday life. Though determined to follow through with my promises made after receiving the prophetic words, it was challenging to say the least. It seemed that the business had more problems than usual that took my time. These demands made it difficult to attend to the needs of my family, especially the teenagers and their myriad of activities. My wife's trouble continued to a greater degree; however, I was no longer chastising her or pressuring her. I was deliberate in trying to be more loving and supportive to her and the family. Realizing that I could not control her drinking issues, I gave her over to God. He had demonstrated that He could handle her situation, as He had been handling mine. I kept reminding myself about the story of the butterfly and how I was warned that this season might be a very slow process. I was determined to continue growing in this newfound spiritual journey and often reflected on how the Venezuelan trip had become a benchmark of my faith. The "lady in the street" experience reminded me of the need for the reverent fear of God that continues to this day.

Returning home from the farm one Saturday afternoon to get a bite to eat, I accidentally walked into a conversation between my daughter and Nita. De'Anne sounded distressed. Her sincerity and love for her mom moved Nita to admit that she needed help. As they continued discussing possible solutions, she insisted that any treatment be private. I stayed quiet, listening. *Could this conversation be the beginning of an answer to our prayers? Is this God's grand design?* I wondered. As their conversation was ending, I went into the kitchen. After eating, I walked to De'Anne's room and asked, "Sweetie, are you okay?"

"Yes, Dad, I'm okay," she answered.

We exchanged "I love you's" as we hugged each other.

Then I walked to our bedroom to check on Nita. Finding her asleep, I wrote a note saying, "I'll be back from the farm around dark. Luv u," and placed it on the nightstand next to her.

Days later, in early morning prayer time, as I was talking to God about my wife's condition. I suddenly saw the names Jason and Ariel in my mind. That's one way God communicates with me. I hear no spoken words, but I "see" a word, phrase, or sometimes even a sentence. I remembered sharing my wife's problem with Jason and Ariel after hearing their testimony. It seems Jason had a brother who had died from alcohol abuse. Also, Ariel had been instantly delivered from addiction to alcohol and drugs. The thought entered my mind to invite them to Texas to minister to my wife. I would have to pray for wisdom on how to approach Nita without alarming her. I thought that having this couple spend time with us might be what Nita needed for breakthrough. Following through with prayers over the next few days, I simply requested of my heavenly Father that if I interpreted His message correctly, then I would, by faith, lay all responses to my invitation at His feet. It would be done in Jesus' name! Amen!

The next night I approached Nita about inviting Jason and Ariel to our house. I did not give her all the details I knew about them, but I mentioned that Ariel had been delivered instantly from substance abuse. I told her I thought she would enjoy Ariel because they had similar personalities. Then related that Jason was quieter and reserved like me. To my surprise, Nita agreed without any hesitation.

"When will they come?" she asked.

"I'll call them tomorrow and see if they can come this month," I replied.

It was all I could do to bridle my enthusiasm and delight. I called Jason and Ariel the next day and brought them up to date about Nita's situation. After their arrival, Jason would later tell me that he was about to decline my invitation when the presence of the Lord visited him. He suddenly knew that he and Ariel had to say yes. He told me that they would arrive the week after next. I almost broke into tears when I heard his words of acceptance.

"Thank you! Thank you!" I said joyfully.

I offered to send him money for the trip, but he said no.

Overwhelmed, I repeated, "Thank you, thank you, Jason. My words are inadequate to express what I'm feeling right now."

The weekend before they arrived, Nita's parents unexpectedly came to visit. I later learned that she insisted that her mother come and stay with us while Jason and Ariel were here. Nita had persuaded her mother to come by telling her that I was bringing friends I had met on the mission trip to gang up on her. I welcomed her parents as if I knew they were coming all along. Her dad left the next day even though I invited him to stay for the week.

Two days later, Jason and Ariel arrived. It was good to see them. Introductions were made. By suppertime, it was as if everybody had known each other for a long time. The next morning Jason rode with me to the farm; thus, I was able to bring him up to date on our situation. I informed him that her mother had arrived because Nita felt she could protect her if we ganged up on her. Jason just laughed, saying, "It's good that Nita's mother is here. Her mother may be a crutch for Nita that needs to be removed."

That night Jason and Ariel shared their testimonies. Jason shared how he discovered faith during the time of his brother's death due to alcohol. Ariel shared her amazing testimony of being instantly delivered from drugs and alcohol.

The next morning, while Wes and De'Anne were at school, I briefly returned home from work. I wanted to check on everyone. With a calm and soothing voice, Jason began by asking Nita, "Do you have a drinking problem?"

She replied, "I don't think so. Why did you ask?"

I was stunned by the directness of the question. I glanced at Nita's mother and saw her eyes had gotten very big, but she didn't say anything, which was unusual for her.

I held my breath, wondering what would happen. Later Ariel told me that when I left for work, Jason had visited with Nita's mom outside alone. He told her point-blank that her daughter didn't have many more months to live if she didn't get help and quit drinking. Jason helped Nita's mom understand the gravity of the situation. Since he had watched his brother die years before, Jason told her that he was going to confront Nita the next time we were all gathered without the children present. "If you love your daughter," he said in earnest, "as I know you do, please listen. Don't try to rescue her. Everyone here loves her and wants the very best for her."

The room was tense. It was uncomfortable, but Jason continued his direct questioning of my wife. He made known that living with his brother made him aware of the symptoms that many often overlook.

He asked my wife in a calm and loving voice, "How long have you noticed the swelling of your face? Do you get tremors or the shakes? Have you found yourself having to drink more to reach the desired 'buzz'?"

Taking her hand and looking intently into her eyes, he went on, "Nita, we all love you. You know your children love you. We have come this week because of our love for you. This is a problem that you cannot solve by yourself. You have tried to stop drinking without success. While treatment centers can provide you with solutions, you must want to help yourself. The good news is that it's never too late. Once you admit to having this problem, you are on your way to recovery."

Nita turned to her mom, looking for help, but her mom said, "He's right, honey. You need to listen to what Jason is saying. We all love you—I love you—and want the best for you."

With shame in her eyes, Nita finally admitted that she needed help, but she didn't want anyone else to know about this. She preferred to be in a solitary situation, but she didn't know how to proceed. Ariel then began to pray, asking all of us to lay our hands on Nita. She prayed earnestly for an instantaneous healing and deliverance of Nita's addiction. When that did not occur, she prayed that God would open the door and reveal the way for Nita's healing. It was a beautiful moment in the presence of our Lord. There was such a gentle manner in the way that Jason and Ariel ministered to Nita. We all gave her a great big hug as the atmosphere relaxed.

Apologizing to the group that I must return to the business, I turned to Nita's mother and told her how much I appreciated that she had come. It was important that she had witnessed all that had happened with her daughter.

Later that night, as Jason and I watched the news at 10:00 pm, an advertisement appeared between one of the breaks. What we heard was literally breathtaking! The timing of God was once again impeccable! A substance abuse and treatment center in a nearby town would open at the end of the month. A well-known director of the program had been hired from another area. He was bringing highly recommended staff from across the nation to make this one of the better treatment centers in East Texas. This program would also include counseling centers for the entire family.

We now knew that Jason and Ariel's coming was not a coincidence, but had been ordained by the very hand of God. Excitement and anticipation filled my spirit as I called the center the next morning. A receptionist answered the phone, and I briefly described my situation. She asked me to hold for a moment; because she knew that the director would desire to speak directly to me.

The conversation with the director lasted for at least 20 minutes. Tears came to my eyes as I expressed my heartfelt thanks for them agreeing to accept my wife into the program the following week. "Her entry will be two weeks before the official opening of the center," the director said, "but my staff will be delighted to have a patient to work with as they finalize the schedules and fine-tune the program."

Isn't God good? Nita was willing to get help on the condition that her participation in a program would be kept confidential. Later that day, we ate lunch while the children were at school. Jason began the conversation by telling our wives about watching the *Ten O'Clock News* the night before. He looked at me to continue telling them what we had seen and heard. I told them about the commercial, my conversation with the director that morning, and how he would accept Nita next week. I shared that she would enter the program two weeks before the program was officially opened, so she would be alone with her participation confidential.

I was encouraged that my wife immediately remarked, "That timing does meet my condition to be all alone."

"Yes," I replied and squeezed her hand, "God's grace and love for you is evident."

"I'll think about it," she said.

Her mother spoke immediately, "Honey, there's no use waiting. This is a perfect opportunity for you to get your life straight."

Nita opened her mouth to object; however, her mother interrupted her and said, "There's no use arguing! I want you to do this. Jason and Ariel telling us about the symptoms you are experiencing reveal to us that time is of the essence."

My wife's resolve wavered. She looked from her mother to me and back to her mother. "Nita," her mother said, patting her hand, "we will do this together. You can do this! You can do anything you set your mind to."

Jason spoke up and said, "The director is awaiting Ferel's phone call to confirm your coming. They will make preparations over this weekend for you to come on Tuesday next week." Then he took her hands into his and looked intently at her with concerned yet loving eyes and said, "How about it?"

"Okay, okay. I'll go!" Nita gave in, "Make your phone call."

As we continued to eat, she raised the question, "What will we do about the children?"

"I've been thinking about that," I replied. "De'Anne begins her first day of summer by attending twirling school. Wes can either stay with me, or I know his grandmother would be more than happy to take him home. We'll all visit with the kids after supper tonight, letting them know of your decision."

Wes and De 'Anne were delighted to know that their mom was going to get help.

"Are you also going to quit smoking?" they both asked.

She laughed and said, "Let's take one step at a time!"

Jason and Ariel left for home the next morning amidst all the hugs and loving goodbyes. My love for them had grown deeper, and I thanked them for coming. Our gratitude went beyond words that we could express.

As they departed, I could not help but marvel at how God continued to orchestrate time, people, and events to bring healing and unity to my family. I was in awe of how He opened my eyes to behold the manifestation of His love through signs, wonders, and miracles! It was no coincidence that everything had fallen into place for Nita! My vision in going to Venezuela had been narrow and self-centered—it was about my spiritual growth, but more! Jason and Ariel were on that mission team for more than they originally thought. God used their past pain and experience to open the heart, mind, soul, and spirit of my wife, her mom, our children, and me. Together, we received the good news of God's love and healing for each of us.

My understanding was slowly beginning to grasp the incredible love and mercy of God! I reflected on the words of the Psalmist, revealing even more about God's love and mercy:

"Many times he delivered them, but they were bent on rebellion and they wasted away in their sin. Yet he took note of their distress when he heard their cry; for their sake he remembered his covenant and out of his great love he relented."[1]

It's just not about one person. It's also about how that one life integrates and affects the lives of others. It's the "grand design of God" for every person, isn't it? It's *"... immeasurably more than all we ask or imagine, according to his power that is at work within us, to Him be glory in the church and in Christ Jesus throughout all generations, forever and ever! Amen."[2]*

We were determined to keep where Nita was confidential for the next 30 days. When asked where my family and wife were, I answered that she and the kids were visiting the grandparents. After a couple of weeks, someone started a rumor in town that we must be getting a divorce. I would chuckle under my breath every time someone mentioned that to me. Then I whispered a quiet prayer, "Thank you, Lord, for healing my wife, my children, her parents, and me through your servants Jason and Ariel. Bless them."

The alcohol treatment center's program lasted for thirty days. During the first week, no visitors were allowed. I saw my wife once the second week and no more than two times each week until the program was over. The next six months saw our family life return to as normal as possible. Nita and I attended counseling every other week, combined with her participation in the 12-step program while I attended the Al-Anon program. Returning home one night, she turned and said, "I know I'm okay. I don't believe it's doing me any good to go to these meetings and keep retelling where I have been in the past. I believe that I am a new person in Christ Jesus. I'm ready to move on from the past, live in the present, and look forward to the future! Don't you agree?"

I responded, "I certainly do, my love! What a wonderful declaration you just made. I'm so happy and proud of what you have accomplished. I love you very much. Yes, God is good!

Yes," she said smiling, "all the time!"

"Then, in your desperate condition, you called out to God. He got you out in the nick of time; He put your feet on a wonderful road that took you straight to a good place to live. So, thank God for His marvelous love, for His miracle mercy to the children He loves."[3]

This Psalm became my wife's favorite Scripture. It's a wonderful demonstration of God's love rescuing and restoring people. The Psalm hints at God's "grand design" for each person's life. His love places them on a wonderful pathway that leads them to a better life. Nita's victory in overcoming addiction was strategic to God's "grand design" of restoring us both. Her addiction began after I resigned the pulpit during our season of dwelling in the "wilderness," and ended there before we reentered ministry together again. God delights in manifesting His love so that each person can walk without stumbling, find purpose without wandering, discover hope without despair, and experience an everlasting love without loneliness. The love, mercy, and sovereignty of our heavenly Father for each person ushers forth **Hope Beyond!** It did for my family, and it will also do the same for you!

ENDNOTES

1. Psalm 106:43-45.
2. Ephesians 3:20b-21.
3. Psalm 107:6-8, MSG.

CHAPTER 12

THOSE TERRIBLE MONDAYS

It had been about eighteen months since my return from Venezuela. Early in September, around noon on a Thursday, my wife and I were working at the business. All the employees had departed for lunch. It was unusual for Nita to still be there, but she was trying to get some business statements finalized for mailing. The telephone ringing disturbed her work and caused me to look up from mine as I sat within my office.

"Who did you say this was?" I heard.

Nita motioned for me to pick up the phone as she said excitedly, "It's a long-distance call from Venezuela with an interpreter. Answer it quick!"

I was as shocked and stunned as she was. Full of excitement and anticipation, I wondered, *Who in the world can that be?* I couldn't help noticing that instead of Nita hanging up the phone and going back to work, she had turned around in her office chair, listening intently to the conversation.

The interpreter began by telling me his first name. He advised that Bethany, who had been our host, was there by his side. Bethany had prophesied over me and said she had a message to give me. I could hear her voice in the background talking to him as he began to interpret her message.

"Last night," she began, "I had a dream about you where I saw your face. You were standing outside in the countryside, and black, dark, ominous clouds were churning in the skies above. This storm was not natural. It was a spiritual attack. It was a satanic storm trying to destroy your maturing faith and newfound understanding."

I gripped the phone tightly, listening with careful attention.

"Have no fear," Bethany declared, "because our heavenly Father is sending angels to oversee you and your house. But there is one thing you must do. She gave me several specific verses of Scripture to declare aloud during my prayer time in the days ahead. Remember that regardless of the situation or circumstance that is happening about you, always declare the praises of our Lord with His Word. It is essential that you do this!"

"I will," I promised, then asked how she was and inquired after the house church where we had been. Bethany replied that she was well and the house church had grown. I thanked her for her obedience to call in warning me. I assured her that Nita and I would do what she asked and begin to prepare spiritually for what might lay ahead. Thanking the interpreter, we said goodbye.

When I hung up the phone, Nita asked, "Was that really the lady you told us about where so much happened at her house?"

"Yes," I replied, "that was her. I'm not sure how to receive everything that we heard?" We both agreed to make sure we praised the Lord in our own way, regardless of what might happen.

Since my wife's healing, any type of spiritual pressure by me was ignored. I was determined to follow prophetic words received from my Christian brothers and sisters in Venezuela as best I could. The Lord would accomplish Nita's continued spiritual understanding. Up until now, the family had continued to join together in weekly worship and monthly attendance at our Business Men's fellowship meetings.

A couple of our employees returned from lunch, so Nita and I decided to go eat together and talk about the unsuspecting and surprising phone call.

The weekend came and passed. Nothing unusual happened. I continued to declare the Scripture verses Bethany had instructed.

Monday came. At 10:15 pm, the phone rang. I stood up from watching *The Ten O'Clock News* and answered, "Hello?"

A man's stern and unemotional voice confirmed my name and address, then said, "I'm sorry to inform you that your son has been run over by a car at the university. He's been taken by ambulance to the emergency room at the hospital. I only know that he was conscious in the ambulance while being attended to. I would urge you and your wife to travel there as soon as possible."

Stunned, I thanked him and hung up.

I was in a state of unbelief. I briskly walked to where Nita was finalizing her preparations for bed. Looking at her intently, I took her hand. She knew instantly that something was wrong since that was an unusual gesture.

"What's wrong?" she asked.

"Our son has been in an accident while walking in a crosswalk at the university," I answered. "He's okay, but has been taken to the emergency room. We need to get there quickly!"

As we were driving onto the highway, she excitedly shouted to me, "Put your praise music on! Let's sing the praise music together as we drive."

She rarely listened to this type of music, but she remembered Bethany's phone call only a few days earlier. As we drove, singing and listening to the praise songs, a sense of calm enveloped us both.

Arriving at the hospital, we walked quickly, then halfway ran to the emergency doors. One of my son's best friends was standing in the corridor. He walked to meet us. He was still excited as he told us that Wes was being attended to by one of the primary doctors who had arrived a few minutes earlier.

"Do you know how it happened?" We asked together as I placed my arm around Nita's shoulder.

"Yes," he replied. "We had been in the library, walking back to the dormitory; there was one street to cross. We were talking as we came to the crosswalk and didn't see any vehicle approaching. Wes had taken a couple of steps in front of me in the crosswalk. Suddenly, this fast-moving car appeared and hit him while barely missing me. The car spun Wes upwards, turning somersaults, where he came down on the top edge of the windshield. He rolled downward, breaking the wiper blade and side mirror on the car. Somersaulting one more time, he fell to the ground hitting his head on the curb."

As his friend was relating the account of the accident, I couldn't help think, *My God, my son should be dead!*

I thought about the recent telephone call from Bethany. For some strange reason, I thought about my survival from falling out of a car at sixty mph at the age of six. Looking upward, I shouted out loud, "Praise God! Praise God! Thank you for your protective angels, Lord."

Looking at Nita, I couldn't help noticing that she had her hand collapsed over her mouth as she listened to Wes' friend—a wonderful young man whom we had known since moving to East Texas—finish his account of the accident. Nita and I hugged him together. We could tell that he was still shaken from the accident, as were we. Nita and I got a cup of coffee from the lounge and bought our young friend his favorite soda. We waited patiently for the doctor's report. We felt somewhat encouraged; because we heard Wes and the doctor talking from the emergency room. Shortly after that, the doctor appeared in the lounge, remarking how fortunate Wes had been not to sustain major and critical injuries. In fact, he said, "I don't normally believe in miracles, but your son might represent one. From the x-rays, we know that he has not sustained any broken bones nor sustained any head injury other than a minor concussion. There has been no swelling of the brain so far, which is very unusual for accidents

I DON'T NORMALLY BELIEVE IN MIRACLES, BUT YOUR SON MIGHT REPRESENT ONE.

of this nature. We will continue to monitor your son closely tonight and tomorrow to make sure that nothing develops. He will be very sore and bruised for several days. All three of you are welcome to visit him in the emergency room. I will make final preparations to have him taken to a hospital room for tonight and the next few days."

All three of us had tears of relief in our eyes as we walked down the corridor to see Wes. Walking into the room, Wes turned to us and said, "Dad, can't you get me out of here?"

Four days later, Wes checked himself out of the hospital to prepare to play in a collegiate tournament with the university golf team. His golf coach could not believe his quick recovery. His soreness, however, did affect his play.

During the next couple of days, Nita and I continued to discuss all that had happened. On the following Sunday evening, right before bedtime, she wanted to share with me some final conclusions that she had realized. Her demeanor reflected greater sensitivity to her spiritual understanding as she talked about her healing from her addiction and this experience. She confessed that she thought I had planned everything on the prior event, but now had become convinced that both events were more than just a coincidence. The call from Bethany was not a coincidence! Her instructions gave specifics.

"Forgive me," she said, "that I threatened to divorce you if you went on that missionary trip. Thank you for going! If you had not gone, our circumstances might've been changed forever. I do not understand nor can I comprehend why God would show you all that He did on that trip."

Pausing, she continued, "Neither do I fully understand how God directed people for my healing. Neither do I understand this miracle for our son's life. I suddenly realized that I didn't need to understand why God's love would be so special for you, myself, and our son. Now I just say, 'Thank you, loving Father. Praise Your holy name!' I heard you say after returning from your trip that you possessed 'benchmarks of faith.' Not really understanding what you meant at that time, I do now because now I possess my own 'benchmarks of faith.'"

Wow! *Hope Beyond!*

The week passed quickly. Wes came home briefly from the golf tournament over the weekend. The family continued to marvel that nothing had been broken and that he hadn't sustained any type of serious injury. Praising and worshipping God was now different for our entire family.

The business was thriving the following Monday morning with many product deliveries. Walk-in customers enjoyed the free coffee while socializing with my employees and friends. Glancing at the clock on the office wall, I noticed it was 11:42 am, almost time for a luncheon appointment. Suddenly, our warehouse plate glass windows vibrated sharply. The building shook as an explosion was heard. We all looked at each other, wondering what had happened. It took only seconds for large, black mushroom clouds to rise in the air. The ringing telephone focused our attention as we heard Nita responding to someone on the phone saying, "Oh my gosh! Thanks for calling."

Turning around, she shouted, "Everyone! Our convenience store on the hill has exploded. It's on fire!"

I quickly turned to an employee and said, "Hop in my truck. Let's go!"

I shouted to my wife, "Please call and cancel my luncheon engagement," as we hurried to my pickup and departed.

Vehicles were already parking along the highway, as traffic had been halted. We ran about one-half of a mile. Reaching the crest of the hill, we could see what was happening. The pump island had flames shooting at least 25 feet into the air. The city's volunteer fire department had responded quickly and was doing a great job. I walked over to the fire chief, who was standing and giving orders at a distance. He explained that someone had forgotten to return the gasoline hose from their car to the pump; thereby, driving off with it. A spark ensued. Explosion! A quick-thinking cashier inside the store heard the explosion and instantly turned the emergency pump switch off. This helped contain the fire and prevent further explosions.

By now, customers and employees had vacated the convenience store and the café attached to the same building. Store and café alike had been fairly full of people since this was the lunch hour and the busiest time of the day. It only took a few minutes for this potentially dangerous fire to be put out. The smell was horrendous as black smoke from hot metal, melted wire, and insulation continued to smolder. Staring at the rubble where gasoline pumps and a canopy once stood, there was now only black rubbish.

As I began to calm down emotionally, I remembered the phone call from Bethany. It had reminded me to praise God as I surveyed the damage. Customers were exiting and entering both the store and the café when the explosion occurred. No one was hurt. I say again—*no one was hurt!* No one was burned. I had witnessed another miracle!

I felt a tap on my shoulder. Turning around, Nita and one of our employees—a very good friend—joined me in surveying the damage. They were both amazed to learn that no one had been hurt. Facing them, I said, "Join with me as I pray to God our Father who has blessed this day in the midst of destruction with no lives being lost and the miracle of life for our son. We continue to praise Your holy name!"

Both women joined me in shouting, "Amen! Hallelujah!"

The rest of the week was uneventful as repairs and restoration began. The store and café looked much better after new pumps, canopy, and a needed paint job had been completed.

It was Sunday evening. The family relaxed, eating their favorite bowl of ice cream. Wondering out loud, I asked my wife, "Do you remember if Bethany said how long the black clouds and storms would last in her vision?"

"Not really," she replied. "One thing I do remember, however, was to keep on praising. Keep on praising, whatever happens! That's a promise! Okay, let's start getting everything together for school and work tomorrow. Who's going to begin the nightly shower routine?"

The third Monday following the phone call arrived. A beautiful sunrise greeted me as I strolled outside. The air was cool and crisp, with a hopeful hint of a changing season. I looked to the heavens and spoke a brief prayer out loud. "Lord, thank You for giving my wife and me a prophetic message from Bethany about the brewing dark and violent storms. Your love for us, in providing that message, gave us the faithful support and stability that we needed at this time."

A tear formed in my eye as I continued, "I confess, Lord, that we are weak and fragile both in our faith and in our family. The loss of our son would have been devastating."

The Spirit of the Lord took me suddenly back in memory to Thanksgiving 1965. Nita was in the hospital in labor about to give birth to our first child. The nurse entered the room, telling me that my dad was calling. He inquired how the birth was progressing and how I was holding up.

"Everything's going well, Dad," I replied.

"That's very good news," he said. Then reluctantly, he continued, "Son, I have some very sad news. I'm sorry to inform you that your grandmother passed away about an hour ago. We started not to call, but your mother wanted you to know."

Pausing to catch my breath, I then replied, "Thank you, Dad. Love you both. I will call later."

The call ended, and I walked back down the hallway. The nurse informed me that my wife was in delivery. It seemed only moments when the nurse reappeared and said that I would be able to go into the room shortly. "I'm sorry to inform you, however," she said, "that your baby was stillborn at delivery. Your wife is okay, though."

Tears were streaming from my eyes as I ran down that hospital corridor, shouting very loud upon reaching the outside, "God, this isn't supposed to happen to preachers!"

"Yes, Lord," I prayed, "that was a very difficult time, especially for my wife. I believe, God, that you brought this memory back to remind me of Your incredible love and grace. You knew, gracious Lord, that my wife and I couldn't endure the devastating loss of our son." Wiping tears from my eyes, I returned to my original prayer, which was praising and thanking Him for all He provided in the midst of these storms.

Nita and I went to lunch at our café on the third Monday. We were relaxing and visiting with customers when sounds of sirens and firetrucks pierced the air! We all rushed out the front door to see the commotion at the bottom of the hill at the service station on the corner. Guess what? It was happening again! I had rented that station and leased it to an operator. I walked down the hill to see what was going on, thinking to myself that, *at least, there was no fire or explosion*. I could see people and my operator walking about, so I assumed no one had been hurt. Approaching, I noticed that a small log truck had crashed into the canopy and front edge of the building missing the fuel pumps. *Thank God, I thought!*

It was unbelievable listening to the truck's driver and my operator tell what happened to the local authorities. The driver had been eating inside the BBQ place on top of the hill across from my store and café. The brakes on his truck released with his load of logs rolling over 100 yards downhill into the station. If a person looked at where the truck had been parked and where the truck had hit the building, it was almost a straight line with only two or three feet clearance on each side of the truck. It rolled downhill, missing several utility poles and lines. Not only that, but the truck also had, with its own momentum, rolled through a paved ditch and street drain, over a small embankment that divided a major thoroughfare, through another paved ditch, and finally rolled into the building fifty yards away! Any person would have difficulty steering an old log truck that straight! With the amount of traffic we have around lunchtime at this traffic circle, it was even more amazing that this truck had not rolled into another moving vehicle. A miracle!

After that incident, our normal activities filled the remainder of the week. A relaxing and pleasant family weekend was spent in Louisiana as we watched my son's golf team play in another tournament. It was good to get away and change the atmosphere.

Awakening the following Monday morning, I rolled over in bed thinking, *I don't want to get up because of events that had occurred over the last three Mondays.*

Nevertheless, I was learning to live one day at a time, walking in faith, and trusting in a heavenly Father whose love orchestrates time, people, and events so that His faithful can partner with Him in bringing His will on earth as it is in heaven. As the sun set that Monday afternoon, the storm clouds had disappeared. We often do not understand the ways of God, but we do believe that *"the Light shines in the darkness, and the darkness has not overcome it."*[1]

WE OFTEN DO NOT UNDERSTAND THE WAYS OF GOD, BUT WE KNOW THAT HIS LIGHT SHINES IN DARKNESS AND CANNOT BE OVERCOME.

Experiencing these three terrible Mondays had enabled our family to grow in faith and love. The family had become both closer and wiser with God and each other in weathering these storms. As I think about it, we witnessed three terrible Mondays be transformed into three Monday miracles by God's marvelous love! That's *Hope Beyond!*

ENDNOTE

1. John 1:5.

CHAPTER 13

$\mathcal{A}$ Pleasant Surprise

How great it was to begin a new week and not have anything strange or drastic happen! Everything that had affected my wife and me these past few weeks also affected our employees. They experienced the added stress, emotional, and physical undertaking that was needed to get the business functioning back to normal.

Every spare moment I had as the week progressed was spent in reflection upon what had happened. There were many spiritual lessons for the family and me to learn together, but the lesson of God's unfailing love was undeniable! His Word, given through Bethany, helped to increase our faith amid the storms taking place.

I meditated on the words of Peter. He said, *"Through our faith, the mighty power of God constantly guards us until our full salvation is ready to be revealed in the last time. May the thought of this cause you to jump for joy, even though lately you've had to put up with the grief of many trials! But these only reveal the sterling core of your faith, which is far more valuable than gold that perishes, for even gold is refined by fire. Your authentic faith will result in even more praise, glory, and honor when Jesus the Anointed One is revealed. You love him passionately although you did not see him, but through believing in him you are saturated within an ecstatic joy, indescribably sublime and immersed in glory."[1]*

In the light of all that happened to us in the last few weeks, who's faith, love in Jesus, and our heavenly Father wouldn't grow immensely? To be a recipient of such love and grace is still incomprehensible, yet humbling in the process. Psalm 23 is familiar to believers and unbelievers alike. The writer, King David, believed that regardless of the valley he faced, the Lord would always be at his side as a loyal Shepherd. Experientially, David knew that they would walk through the valley of the shadow of death together. Like King David, experiencing the awesome power and love of God, difficult circumstances will deepen and expand your core of faith into solid bedrock that becomes immovable. Yes, my times of reflection revealed a newfound depth of my faith.

WHEN WE EXPERIENCE THE AWESOME POWER AND LOVE OF GOD, DIFFICULT CIRCUMSTANCES WILL DEEPEN AND EXPAND OUR CORE OF FAITH INTO SOLID BEDROCK THAT BECOMES IMMOVABLE.

One evening, the family shared their day while eating a bowl of their favorite ice cream when the phone rang. I was pleasantly surprised to hear the voice of my Floridian friend and roommate from the Venezuelan mission trip, Andrew. He quickly related that the purpose of his call was to invite my wife and me to go on another Venezuelan trip at the end of October. This trip would only be for five days. They still had several openings to fill. Then he told me that Jason and Ariel had signed up and were hoping that Nita and I would also come. I told him that I would get back with him in a day or two.

Hanging up the telephone, I returned to the family and my bowl of melting ice cream.

"Who was it, Dad?" De'Anne inquired.

I was getting somewhat excited as I relayed the message and invitation that Andrew extended. Nita's first response was that it might be difficult for us both to go since it was during school. I thought that was encouraging since she didn't just say no. We continued discussing Andrew's proposal when De'Anne offered, "With all that has recently happened, I believe this would be a great trip for both you and mom, especially mom. Call your folks, Dad, and see if they will come stay with us since you guys will only be gone a short time. You guys would have great fun seeing your friends from Florida as well as being able to see Bethany, who gave you God's prophetic word before all those 'terrible Mondays.'"

What's that old saying that wisdom comes out of the mouth of babes? Our daughter seemed to hit all the right reasons for going! Nita turned, smiling at me, and said, "Providing your folks can come and keep the kids, let's go!"

"Okay then," without any objection, I said, "I'm going to call Andrew, tell him that we will go, and get the details needed to make flight reservations."

"Before you make that call," my wife spoke out, "let me and De'Anne call your folks to make sure they will keep the kids."

"Great idea," I replied.

Grandmother and granddad were only too happy to have an excuse to come to visit. My dad always enjoyed working around livestock. He was thrilled to know that he would watch over the farm while we were gone.

The next night, Nita and I called Jason and Ariel, sharing our decision to travel to Venezuela together. Excitement grew as we all looked forward to our reunion.

The next few weeks passed quickly as we prepared for our journey together. I felt in my spirit that this shared experience would deepen our relationship and my wife's faith. I was especially excited that Nita would have the opportunity to witness, firsthand, the kinds of signs, wonders, and miracles that I had experienced on my first trip. In lifting her in prayer before the trip, one phrase repeatedly came to my mind. The phrase was that God was going to "knock the socks off my wife!" I know that sounds funny, but that's what I sensed.

Having concluded our first day in Venezuela, Andrew had been correct in saying that this mission trip would not be as intense as the first one. The day's events consisted of our mission team ministering to local chapter officers and their wives. Nightly banquets were still held for outreach. A delightful event was planned later in the week for an all-day tour that would take us to an alpine village for lunch. We drove into the gorgeous countryside revealing snow on distant mountain peaks. It was a beautiful and relaxing trip made with delightful friends.

Nita slept in the next morning and dined by herself at breakfast. Her experience at breakfast was one of those funny-but-not-so-funny times. She seemingly had forgotten my warnings about how strong Venezuelan coffee was.

"Drink it with half cream and half coffee," I had advised.

When we came back in the afternoon, Jason and I went to find our wives. They were in the back corner of the lobby laughing and giggling. I couldn't help but notice, as I approached Nita, that her face seemed flushed. She was on a "high," laughing quite loud and uncontrollably at times. The other wives had us sit as Ariel told the story to us. It seems Nita couldn't understand why the waiter kept bringing only a small cup of coffee. Ariel began laughing as she tried to imitate my wife gesturing for a regular-sized cup of coffee. He finally brought it to her, and Nita refused the cream! She sat there over the next hour eating breakfast while drinking at least three regular-sized cups of the strong Venezuelan coffee. Bursting out laughing again, Nita couldn't remember whether she drank three cups or more! She was "high," all right! It was a wonder that they hadn't called the doctor. That caffeine "high" lasted until lunchtime the next day. She had not been able to sleep either. Needless to say, Nita learned her lesson. She became the talk of the team. I don't think that's what was meant; however, when I felt that God would "knock her socks off," but she almost did it on her own!

A highlight of the trip for us both was joining Jason and Ariel to attend a women's gathering at a beautiful beach house. We each gave a short testimony. I was so proud of my wife when she gave her testimony. Nita told how God delivered her from alcohol with the help of these Floridian friends standing by her. It was so heartfelt, simple, and sincere. The presence of the Lord was very strong in the room. Many of the women had tears flowing freely down their cheeks. My tears were tears of joy! What a transformation I witnessed as she spoke for the first time in public. She "knocked the socks off me!" She was the last to speak.

The leader then invited anyone that wanted prayer to come forward. Our wives began praying for them. Singing broke out after the prayer session. Five or six Venezuelan women that Nita had prayed for surrounded her as we all continued to sing. Suddenly, one of the women at her side broke out singing in her prayer language, falling to the floor. My wife didn't move a muscle. She just listened and watched. It was a beautiful melody, spiritually moving us all to tears. The singer paused briefly. Then began singing again in English, interpreting what she had just sung in Spanish. Afterward, she said that she didn't speak English. Amazing! I believe that was a unique sign and wonder from God, given for my wife that truly "knocked her socks off." Nita would never forget that experience! I wish we could've recorded it, but there were no iPhones then.

It seemed that we had just arrived in Venezuela when the trip ended and we were returning home. In retrospect, every mission trip is unique in its experiences shared. This trip was memorable in a personal way and special in the bonding of our faith as a couple. It was remarkable to reunite with Bethany, who prophesied over me on the first trip and had called with the words of warning. Nita and I both cherished our time with Bethany as we expressed our deepest gratitude. We also testified to her how we witnessed those terrible Mondays becoming Monday miracles!

Sharing the journey with Andrew, Jason, and Ariel, who had been so influential in the progress of our faith, made it even more precious. Most of all, witnessing my wife being transformed and growing in her faith was a sign, wonder, and miracle all its own.

After saying goodbyes with our friends at the Miami airport, we departed for home. Nita expressed how she now understood why I didn't want to come home after my first trip.

She continued, "This trip has been so eye-opening to the wonders of our Lord. To meet such amazing Christians in Venezuela, who worship under difficulty at times, inspires me to be a more faithful servant of my Lord."

Peter's epistle came to mind as we relaxed and traveled towards home. The depth of his written words brought fresh meaning as we read them:

> "If you bow low in God's awesome presence,
> he will eventually exalt you as you
> leave the timing in His hands.

> Pour out your all your worries and stress upon Him and leave
> them there, for He always tenderly cares for you.

> Be well balanced and always alert, because your enemy,
> the devil, roams around incessantly, like a roaring lion
> looking for its prey to the devour.

> Take a decisive stand against him and resist his every attack
> with strong, vigorous faith. For you know that
> your believing brothers and sisters around the world are
> experiencing the same kinds of troubles you endure.

> And then, after your brief suffering, the God of all loving grace,
> who has called you to share in his eternal glory in Christ,
> will personally and powerfully restore you
> and make you stronger than ever.

> Yes, he will set you firmly in place and build you up.

> And he has all the power needed to do this—forever! Amen."[2]

Nita and I were learning how to live life by standing with a strong and vigorous faith. We were learning to respond in times of difficulty with praise by believing in a God who walks by our side through every valley. We were growing in our dependency on Him by believing in a God who has the power to restore and make us stronger in Him, especially in our weakness.

The words of this old hymn came to mind:

"What a fellowship, what a joy divine,
leaning on the everlasting arms;

what a blessedness, what a peace is mine,
leaning on the everlasting arms.

Oh, how sweet to walk in this pilgrim way,
leaning on the everlasting arms;

Oh, how bright the path grows from day to day,
leaning on the everlasting arms.

What have I to dread, what have I to fear,
leaning on the everlasting arms;

I have blessed peace with my Lord so near,
leaning on the everlasting arms."[3]

We were in the process of spiritual transformation in learning how to live our faith by leaning on His everlasting arms and in the conviction of **Hope Beyond.**

ENDNOTES

1. 1 Peter 1:5-8 TPT.
2. 1 Peter 5:6-11 TPT.
3. From the hymn, "Leaning on the Everlasting Arms." United Methodist Hymnal. Book of United Methodist Worship, copyright 1989, The United Methodist Publishing House, Twenty-Ninth Printing—2007 pg. 133.

CHAPTER 14

$\mathcal{S}$TEP BY $\mathcal{S}$TEP

*"But the moment one turns to the Lord with an open
heart, the veil is lifted and they see.
Now, the 'Lord' I'm referring to is the Holy Spirit, and
wherever he is Lord, there is freedom.
We can all draw close to him with the veil removed from
our faces. And with no veil, we all become like mirrors who
brightly reflect the glory of the Lord Jesus.
We are being transfigured into his very image as we move
from one brighter level of glory to another.
And this glorious transformation comes from the Lord,
who is the Spirit."*

2 CORINTHIANS 3:16-18 TPT

We returned home from Venezuela to excited children and grandparents who were eager to hear what all took place. They listened intently as Nita shared her thoughts and feelings. They heard a testimony similar to the one she had shared with the Venezuelan women. She related how the young girl began singing a song in the Spirit and then gave the interpretation of the song in English. Since my parents and children had not been raised in this type of spiritual atmosphere, it was difficult for them to understand what really took place. Likewise, though we did not fully understand the ways by which God chose to manifest His presence, it's easier to accept when you witness what takes place. What was important to my parents and children was the change they saw in my wife as she shared her stories.

As before, reality sets in very soon after returning from a trip. Anyone might think that life would instantly change or be different immediately due to all the recent events and understanding that had taken place. I wish that had been the case, but it wasn't. Old habits and patterns are hard to break. For whatever reason, we sometimes continue to do what we know not to do and do not do what we should be doing.[1] The competitive demands of business continued. Our family structure would soon change again with De'Anne preparing to enter college. Regardless of what was transpiring, however, my "benchmark of faith" would always rest upon the events of that first Venezuelan mission trip in 1984, where God manifested Himself in ways that I could never imagine. He reawakened my heart as a shepherd. The second trip, which I shared with Nita, strengthened her spiritual foundation. This trip became a "benchmark of faith" for her. She also believed that God gave her a special gift in reuniting us with Jason and Ariel, who helped in her healing process from addiction.

The second trip confirmed my growing conviction that I described as having a lot of garbage to clean up before entertaining the thought of returning to the pulpit. The second trip brought a newfound understanding as a couple that would lead to a continuous process of becoming "God chasers." Anytime we heard that the Spirit of God was moving in a revival or at a house church meeting, we would be there. We also continued to support the Business Men's fellowship by helping organize a chapter in our local community. This allowed the opportunity to provide businessmen and businesswomen testimonies for anyone to hear and participate.

In November 1987, Nita and I were invited again to join a Floridian team going back to Venezuela for a third time. My main interest in going would be to share the experience with a close friend, a local pastor, and his wife. I felt they would greatly benefit from witnessing signs, wonders, and miracles. I had come to realize how much God blessed me during the first trip. His desire was for me to now experience a greater joy by sharing this blessing with others.

Nita was unable to go, but she encouraged me to make the trip. I believe the hand of God was upon my three invitees because they agreed to go. Whatever they needed spiritually, I knew that God would not disappoint them.

As departure for the trip approached, my excitement grew. This trip would provide a similar itinerary to the first trip. The first meeting in Maracaibo didn't disappoint anyone as the presence of God was manifested with more than 50 people accepting Jesus as their Savior. Healings occurred as people sat in their seats. Following the meeting, we were mingling with the people when someone grabbed my arm. Turning around, I saw a young lad I did not recognize because he had grown so much. It was Jesse, the young man that I had given my belt buckle to in 1984. What a joyful and emotional reunion to see him and his dad! As I heard their brief testimony about what God had done for their family since we first met, a greater blessing ensued.

I was looking forward to worshiping the next morning as the entire group returned to La Cruce. The church was just outside

Maracaibo. It was where the young mother had brought her sick baby to me at the altar for a prayer of healing.

I couldn't believe my eyes as I beheld the church. No longer an open tent, it was now an enclosed inflated canvas dome covering a space one and a half times as long and as wide as a football field. Huge blowers circulated the air and enabled this structure to stay inflated. The pastor told us that over 1,000 people were in attendance that morning.

It was a happy day for the pastor and his wife, who journeyed with me. He spoke. She sang. The director of our group asked me to give a ten-minute testimony. The Holy Spirit led me to talk about friendships made and the importance of love in all relationships. I then briefly stated how God had healed my marriage by delivering my wife from addiction and me from pride. After others had spoken, the invitation was given that anyone who desired to be baptized in the Holy Spirit would come forward. Amazingly, at least 300 people walked to the altar. The entire width of the stage at the front was completely jammed with young and old people standing elbow to elbow.

The pastor prayed. The Holy Spirit engulfed everyone. Each person received their prayer language. I was witnessing the day of Pentecost! It was unbelievable! Being caught up in this moment, I arose from my seat on the stage and descended to the floor level. I began to walk amongst the people. The presence and love of the Lord were so strong, causing tears to flow effortlessly. I was overcome with joy unspeakable! Different languages and dialects were heard. Suddenly, I heard a person speaking in English, *"Glory to God in the highest and peace on earth, good will towards men."*

The person paused and opened their eyes. Curiosity overwhelmed me. I touched him on the arm and asked, "Speak English, Señor?"

"No, speak English," he replied. *Wow! Amazing!*

The rest of the trip was filled with many signs, wonders, and miracles. Every event reflected the love and power of God orchestrating time, people, and events that enabled the faithful to partner with Him in bringing His Kingdom and will to earth.

Two final observations were made as this third and final trip to Venezuela concluded. First, I believe everyone is called and sent on these trips for particular purposes that only the Lord can reveal. Secondly, when two people minister together, it's amazing how one and then the other will be given spiritual insight to speak. I believe this is due to how God uses the spiritual giftings of each person; since no one, except Jesus, possesses all these gifts. Therefore, we're sent out two by two, just as in the days when Jesus sent forth His disciples.

The words of Paul found in his letter to the church in Philippi seem appropriate: *"Whatever you have learned or received or heard from me, or seen in me—put it into practice. And the God of peace will be with you."*[2] This confirms experientially, ***Hope Beyond!***

ENDNOTES

1. Romans 7:15.
2. Philippians 4:9.

CHAPTER 15

LESSONS FROM THE OTTERS

Most of us expect God to teach us the principles of life through events like mission trips, community volunteer service projects, church, and other "spiritual" venues. Sometimes, however, God will use or create a spectacular or mundane event to gain our attention. God used a freshwater, furry creature known as the otter, which is related to the weasel, to teach me about an issue in my life that I had not dealt with completely but needed to.

A few months after returning from my third mission trip, the local United States Soil and Conservation District Director held a county meeting for anyone interested in growing catfish. My farm of a hundred and seventy-five acres was unusual in that I had an abundance of water. In years previous, I had built three ponds. These were needed to control excess water from seeping springs. A small canal connected them to a fourth pond that would allow the overflow to drain into the adjacent creek running along my property line. The director explained that the federal government and the state were working together to improve the East Texas economy by hoping to build a catfish processing plant nearby in the next two to three years. Of course, they would need suppliers of catfish to make it happen. Several of us pledged our support and were given sources where we could purchase baby channel catfish 6-8" long. During the next two-plus years, my family and I would spend countless evenings going to the farm and feeding the catfish. We preferred providing the floating catfish food so we could watch them eat. They became like pets, coming to the water's surface whenever they heard the familiar sound of the pickup's engine as we drove up. Standing at the edge of the pond, we would shake the pellets in the can. They would respond with grunting and gurgling noises as they swam towards us.

Several of us growers became concerned that we had not heard anything about the progress being made to build a fish processing plant nearby. The director scheduled another meeting, promising to give us an update. The night of the meeting brought discouraging news as the U.S. government had cut the processing plant from its budget. The state did not have the funds to finance the project by itself. The director was apologetic, but there was nothing he could do.

He provided sources in the state of Mississippi to contact. They would buy our fish and take them to their processing plant. At this time, the state of Mississippi was the leading producer and processor of catfish. I discovered to my dismay, that the price they offered for my catfish was ridiculous. It was as if I was paying them to pick up my fish for nothing. It was easy to understand. It was not feasible for them to buy fish in Texas and haul them to Mississippi.

Since I had a retail convenience store and a small café in the community, I decided to supply them both with my fish. This idea excited me! I began to advertise a gala opening to serve catfish dinners at the café and sell fresh catfish at my store's meat market. At times my imagination would run wild. I envisioned that this might be the beginning of a franchise opportunity. I considered enlisting all the local growers to help.

The opening event was set on a Monday evening, giving me the weekend to catch and process the fish. I had decided to feed them only one time in the previous week so that they would be hungry and easy to catch. The ponds were full of fish. We estimated the largest weighed between 14 to 16 pounds each. Enlisting the help of four friends who had seines, we arrived that Saturday morning with great excitement and expectation. We decided to seine a smaller and narrower pond first. Two men entered the water and proceeded to walk down each edge. They pulled the net up after walking about 10 feet. I was literally shocked to see no fish in the net.

I asked them, "Is the net heavy enough to stay on the bottom of the pond as you walked forward?

"Yes," they replied, "the seines are okay. We'll try again."

This time before the men began, they had the other two men walk towards them from the opposite side of the pond. This strategy should drive the fish towards their net. Accomplishing this, they began to seine once again with the same result. NO FISH! I was beside myself! I didn't know what to do! I suggested that we go to another pond that was connected with the canal. Perhaps the fish had moved. As the two men who had helped stir up the fish from the other direction were getting out of the water, one of them suddenly shouted, "I think I found the problem.

Otters may have gotten into your ponds. See those trails leading down the bank into the water?"

Sure enough, we saw trails running up and down on these two ponds. Upon closer examination, we discovered catfish bones scattered all along the bank, accompanied by piles of otter poop. The remaining ponds reflected the same sad story. My four friends expressed their disappointment for me as they left, driving back to town.

Still not convinced by what we had discovered, I returned to every pond again, hoping for a different result. There was no response from the catfish when I drove up or when I threw the food. This was a very depressing and disheartening moment!

I sat down at the last pond and began to have a huge pity party! My catfish pets were gone. Dreams of becoming a new 'catfish king' had vanished. Those pesky otters had eaten approximately 14,000 pounds of catfish in ten days! Unbelievable! Suddenly in the midst of my pity party, a verse was emblazoned on my mind: *"Do not lay up for yourselves treasures on earth, where moth and rust destroy and where thieves break in and steal; but lay up for yourselves treasures in heaven where neither moth nor rust destroys and where thieves do not break in and steal. For where your treasure is, there your heart will be also."[1]*

Really, Lord? ... Thieves? ...Otters?

I felt the presence of God descend upon me in that moment. Tears flowed as these words from Matthew struck like a two-edged sword. Another verse came to mind: *"To all the rich of this world, I command you not to be wrapped in thoughts of pride over your prosperity, or rely on your wealth, for your riches are unreliable and nothing compared to the living God. Trust instead in the one who lavishes upon us all good things, fulfilling our every need."*[2]

Through otters, God was letting me know that I had not made the progress needed in my spiritual growth and transformation. It was like a helmsman who had gotten off course in steering the ship and was now being corrected severely by the captain. God personally placed the ship back on its proper course.

> GOD USED OTTERS TO SHOW ME THAT I HAD NOT MADE THE PROGRESS NEEDED IN MY SPIRITUAL GROWTH.

Events began to flood my mind over the next two hours. I quickly recapped major events since the "lady in the street" experience in 1981. I had confessed and repented several times about leaving the pulpit with a desire to make money. This feeling, however, had raised the deeper issue: *Would I depend upon God for my needs, or would I depend upon my own resources?* Wasn't this the basic, age-old question that drove Adam and Eve from the garden of Eden where God had provided their every need? I assessed God's unmistakable guidance:

- It was no accident that God sent "the lady in the street" that turned my life around 180°.

- It was no accident when I knew that I had to go on that first mission trip to Venezuela.

- The reality of God was confirmed to me with signs, wonders, miracles, and prophetic anointing.

- It was no accident that my pastor's heart was reawakened when I discovered a personal Jesus of the heart instead of a Jesus of the mind.

- It was no accident that I would meet a Floridian couple who would later provide a healing gateway for my addicted wife to be healed.

- It was no accident that a Venezuelan lady had called to warn us of the terrible Mondays and how to respond in praise regardless.

- It was no accident that my son had lived instead of dying when the car ran over him.

- It was no accident that the second Venezuelan trip bonded my wife and me as one in the Spirit of God.

As I remembered these things, I turned over from my sitting place to lay prostrate in the dirt, repenting and confessing not only my sins; but also a continuing need for God's forgiveness, direction, and guidance.

During the next six years, I would remember this again and again. I tried to sell the distributor business twice. Each sale reached the day of closing only to be canceled without reason. Whereas other jobbers in the area could buy and sell property for profit, all of my property sold for just enough money to cover cleanup expenses. Finally, the business closed its doors in 1993. The warehouse was sold to the highest bidder to pay property taxes owed. During this process, I felt the personal humiliation, guilt, sting, and hurt of disappointing friends by not being able to fulfill financial obligations. Amazingly, though there was no financial gain, God's love, grace, and mercy covered my family and me in every way.

The challenges of family life continued as Nita had a bout with cancer, but thankfully, she was healed after two and half years of treatment. Wes spent four years in college playing golf on a college scholarship. Afterward, he joined the Air Force serving his country for four years. He returned, finishing his college degree. De'Anne graduated from college in four years and then married.

Through it all, however, leaning upon my heavenly Father became routine. God, my companion, was at my side walking me through each valley and helping me provide resources to meet every need. I believed that I had learned the lesson received by God through the otters. My wife and I were living life being dependent upon Him more and more. Though I would still have anxious and stressful moments, our benchmarks of faith would keep us anchored and focused through every storm encountered.

What God's judgment closed on one hand; His mercy opened on the other. As one season closed, another opened, ushering in a fresh sense of **Hope Beyond.**

ENDNOTES
   1. Matthew 6:19-21, NKJV.
   2. 1 Timothy 6:17 TPT.

WHAT GOD'S JUDGMENT CLOSES
ON ONE HAND, HIS MERCY
OPENS ON THE OTHER.

CHAPTER 16

REVELATION OF TWENTY-SEVEN

There seems to be a time of transition whenever one season closes in our life, and a new one begins. My desire to return to the pulpit had grown immensely over the last few years. Still, I knew that I had to do everything possible to terminate the business to focus upon being a pastor again. Finally sensing that the time was right, I made an appointment in late October 1993 to see the district superintendent that presided over this area. Hiram lived in a neighboring town. I knew that two basic questions would be asked. Why did you leave the pastorate, and why do you desire to return? Spending time in prayer before I went, I concluded that I would be true to my testimony, even though Hiram might find some of it strange due to his religious background. One verse in Revelation was key in my thought process: *"And they overcame him by the blood of the Lamb, and by the word of their testimony, and they loved not their lives unto the death."*[1]

My testimony of how I had experienced a Damascus Road event from the "lady in the street" and my first mission trip to Venezuela had become my unshakable "benchmarks of faith." Even though there were still aspects of it that I couldn't comprehend or understand, I would never deny what I had witnessed. The interview lasted over three hours as the superintendent listened intently to my every detail. Leaning forward on his desk and making direct eye contact with me as I finished, I was overjoyed when I heard him say, "Ferel, even though some of your experience was very unique, I am convinced of your heartfelt conviction and passion."

Hiram concluded the interview by telling me about the process of transferring my credentials, since I had served previously in another conference. He told me to go home and pray some more about returning to the pulpit. He would contact me in a few days. He wanted to think and pray about all that I had said.

Sincerely thanking him for his time, I left his office, lifting my voice in praise and thanksgiving for this man of God. Sensing his openness to the workings of the Holy Spirit, I felt an immediate, spiritual kinship with him. Driving home, my prayer was simple, "Lord, I've done all I can do. I place this matter into Your hands. May Your will be done on earth as it is in heaven. Amen."

I was pleasantly surprised when I received a call from him around mid-morning the next day. Hiram related to me that he considered himself to be a born-again man of faith. He believed that God had a unique relationship with every believer who welcomed Him into their heart. Then he said, "Begin the process of transferring your credentials. We'll see what develops. Call me if you have any further questions. Keep me posted about your progress with the other conference where you served."

It took a day or two to get all my information together. One evening early in November, I sat down and began to write my intentions and requests for their assistance to the district office where I had officially retired from. I could not discover who the district superintendent was over that particular area. As I was writing, I felt a strong impression on my mind that it was almost twenty-seven years ago that I had written a letter to resign from the pulpit. Pausing for a moment, I reflected on that timeline. If I were to be appointed to a church in June 1994, it would be twenty-seven years after my resignation. One might even say that I had dwelt in the wilderness for twenty-seven years before being able to cross over to the Promised Land. If reinstated to the pulpit, the first twenty-seven years of my life would have been season one and the next twenty-seven years would be season two, ending in 1994.

Over a week had passed without any response to my letter. Hearing De'Anne answer the house phone around 8:00 pm, I assumed one of her friends was calling. She entered the den and said, "Dad, there's a man on the phone who wants to speak to you. He didn't give me his name."

"Okay," I replied, "thanks."

Saying hello, the man on the other end identified himself. Was I surprised! It was Stephen—a dear friend and former seminary classmate. In 1965, we graduated from the same seminary class, were ordained together, and were appointed to serve in the same conference. To my amazement, he was currently the district superintendent in the area where I had resigned. He was elated that I was returning to serve the local church. If I desired, he offered to find me an appointment in his district. Thanking him for his generous offer, I told him that I thought it best for my family to stay in the conference area where we now resided. Understanding my reasoning, he gave me the good news that he would handle all the necessary paperwork. He would also communicate with Hiram, the district superintendent where I had interviewed. We then caught each other up about our families and hoped to get together soon. Thanking him for all his help, we said goodbye.

Hanging up the phone, I remained at the table. Breathing a sigh of relief, the past few years flashed before my eyes. God had orchestrated time, people, and events all along the way to restore what had been lost. It seemed so surreal! No one could out plan God. The phone call from Stephen was a perfect scenario and confirmed to me that I was proceeding within God's will. Even these two superintendents were the final pieces to complete the process of returning to the pulpit. The timing of God is exact! This was a very emotional moment for me. I knew in my heart that I would be appointed to a pastorate in June 1994.

I was elated and overjoyed as I shared the news with Nita! Since it was still early in the process, we both thought it best not to tell Wes and De'Anne yet. I barely slept that night, as I eagerly awaited the next morning. Contacting Hiram, his secretary informed me that he would be attending meetings until midafternoon.

Hiram returned my call and said, "Ferel, I have already spoken to my colleague and your friend, Stephen. He spoke very highly about you. Everything is on 'go' to complete the transfer process."

We set an appointment to meet in early January to discuss further procedures in approving my request and his recommendation.

During the conference meeting in late May 1994, I was officially approved to transfer, voted into membership of the conference, and appointed to pastor a church within 30 miles from home.

God is so good! He clearly intervened by orchestrating time, people, and events, thus becoming our... **Hope Beyond!**

ENDNOTE

1. Revelation 12:11, KJV.

CHAPTER 17

⅓ New Season

Mixed emotions increased the week before my first appearance in the pulpit after twenty-seven years of absence. Excitement and expectation were combined with anxiousness and self-doubt, all at the same time. *Can I be the pastor the people need to everyone's satisfaction?* I wondered.

As the Sunday came to deliver that first message at my new church appointment, I experienced all these feelings and more! *Would my sermon be relevant?* Some of these people knew me because they were customers in my distributor business. Others were acquainted due to participation in various golf tournaments. I concluded that there was no other way to begin other than to start by sharing my "benchmarks of faith." I was an overcomer by the blood of the Lamb and by the word of my testimony. Why did I leave the pulpit, and why did I return? It all began with the "lady in the street." That testimony would become my introductory message at four other appointments until retiring in 2009.

The Lord really blessed me in that first appointment through a member of the congregation. He was a retired pastor who had much wisdom and a great sense of humor. He became my confidant who assisted me greatly in my transition back to the pulpit after twenty-seven years.

I would always possess a feeling of gratitude towards Hiram, the district superintendent who helped with my new beginning. He retired from the conference, and Gideon, another biblical and faithful man, followed him. Gideon and his wife were spiritually mature, and he was well equipped for senior leadership. This man became my friend and mentor. A close relationship developed. Perhaps, it was due to earlier pastoral ministry and the maturity gained by working in the corporate world. Nita and I had the privilege of serving wonderful people at five churches over the next fifteen years. Each church had its challenges as well as its joys and rewards. The Lord desires to give good gifts to His children. I believe He truly honored us in our commitment to turn our lives 180°. Each church appointment was an advancement and blessing in serving the needs of the people.

Before our retirement, we had spent two years looking for a place to spend our final season of life. As an answer to our prayers and hopes, we discovered an affordable retirement community that was within an hour's drive to either of our moms' homes. Both our dads had passed away. We were fortunate to purchase a home and rent it back to the dweller. She continued to live there until we retired. What a blessing received! We felt God had directed this purchase!

Retiring, we engaged in activities we both enjoyed, until our new season was suddenly turned upside down. A doctor discovered a malignant tumor in Nita's throat and passageway to her lung during a routine physical and X-ray in November 2010. Her cancer in the early 90s had come back with a vengeance.

This tumor was classified as stage 4. We were fortunate to have proficient medical facilities in a nearby metropolitan area less than one hour from our home. It was difficult to comprehend that she would have a full laryngectomy surgical procedure in just three weeks, taking away her ability to speak using her vocal cords. Immediately, a call went out to all our prayer warriors for a healing miracle like we both had witnessed in Venezuela. Unfortunately, it was not to be. We continued to raise our praise and remain strong in our faith. We spent the next year engaged in making numerous trips for her radiation. Nita learned how to speak through her throat stoma. We were blessed amid all her adversity to be able to celebrate our fiftieth wedding anniversary with friends who came from far and wide. She was still the 'belle of the ball'!

I grieved over the loss of her laughter; yet, her determined effort to speak again uplifted my resolve to be a smiling, positive support for her at all times. As any caretaker will attest, during their loved one's final days, an inner strength arises within us to perform and support them in ways we never thought possible. For me, my inner strength arose from a deep abiding faith and a loving heavenly Father. I personally do not know how anyone can go through times like this without a faith that offers **Hope Beyond.**

For both of us, our faith in a loving God continued as we believed He accompanied us through this valley. Her needs, however, became more than I could provide for. Our hospice nurse suggested a nearby private home that would offer 24/7 care. Guilt tended to

OUR FAITH IN A LOVING GOD CONTINUED AS WE BELIEVED HE ACCOMPANIED US THROUGH THE VALLEY OF OUR GRIEF.

overwhelm me. It helped my feelings somewhat that she readily agreed to the move. I still felt, however, that I had let her down. We both felt that God provided a blessing for her as the private home was empty. She would be the only patient residing there for the moment. Two weeks later, all her family and loved ones gathered on Palm Sunday weekend to surprise her. Amazingly, she joined in the festivities and basked in the gorgeous sunlight. She watched the grandchildren play, heard their laughter, and felt love all around. It was a wonderful time. She continued to fight a courageous battle with a constant smile on her face until she realized her ultimate healing on April 7, 2012, when God took her home.

Nita was full of life and laughter. She brought joy to everyone she met. I truly felt that I had experienced losing her twice. The first time was when she lost her voice, and I was unable to hear her laughter. The second time, of course, was when her breath was no more and life ceased.

That's the time when the reality of finality hits. I discovered the truth of remarks made by former parishioners that no person can prepare for such a time as this. All the training of my pastoral ministry made me think that I could, but I couldn't. There's something unexplainable about the reality of finality when that last breath is taken, and that person you loved is no more forever.

I have had very few "'God dreams" in full color. Sometime, predawn Easter morning, on April 8, 2012, I had one. I dreamed this:

> *I was driving my car with a masculine figure sitting in the passenger seat. I saw a distant figure approaching the vehicle through the windshield. The figure was wearing a white skirt with what appeared to be red, small poke-a-dots on it. As the figure continued to walk closer to*

*me, I suddenly saw Nita's face. She was twirling
her white dress. As she walked, I became aware
that her dress was stained with the blood of our
Lord. She walked right up to the car holding her
arms and hands out as if an invitation to join her.*

It was so real and breathtaking that I awoke with a start. I heard myself say, "I love you, but I'm not ready to go yet."

Continuing to lay in the bed, reflecting upon what I had dreamed, I thanked God for giving me the assurance that she was in His presence. Attending Easter service provided additional solace and peace that I was seeking.

During the ensuing days, my emotions were all over the place, similar to riding a roller coaster. There were times when I felt like I was just going through the motions; especially during the funeral visitation, the memorial service, and the gravesite. In the days following, when my family and friends left, I felt so all alone. It takes a period of readjustment when loss occurs. Rescheduling is necessary, especially for those who have been in the role of a caretaker. The routine of feeding tube feedings, dispensing medicine, attending to the personal needs of your loved one, and giving daily reports to those who call occupy the caretaker 24/7. Sleep alludes us as we wait for the slightest movement or ringing of a bell. Their needs are more than the needs of a newborn child. It becomes a consuming labor of love.

My early morning walks were restored, and I often quoted this Psalm:

*"I will lift up mine eyes unto the hills, from whence
cometh my help. My help cometh from the Lord, which
made heaven and earth."*[1]

Reflecting back, feelings of gratitude and thankfulness arose for the empathy expressed by the hospice team, medical professionals, and funeral home personnel who assisted in the final services. Comfort and support were provided by pastors, the community of faith, and beloved friends.

How could love for De'Anne and her family living nearby, and Wes and his family who lived far away, grow any deeper than it already was? But it does! The love of family becomes paramount with every passing day!

Having experienced the loss of a loved one, I believe that grief is unique for every person. How that person reacts to their loss is distinct from everyone else. Most of all, however, was my thankfulness to an abiding, loving heavenly Father who had restored my "benchmarks of faith" years earlier. Together, everything mentioned above helped me to accept this aspect of life that enabled me to walk through this valley of the shadow of death knowing His love, resurrection, and *Hope Beyond!*

ENDNOTE

1. Psalm 121:1-2 KJV.

RESTORATION

Every person will experience grief sooner or later if they live long enough. Though it paused my spiritual journey at first, losing Nita after fifty years of marriage brought a maturity in my spiritual knowledge and understanding that I lacked before.

I have always believed, and still do, that God makes right in heaven what has gone so drastically wrong in this fallen world. You cannot prepare for it. You cannot measure your loss against the loss of anyone else. Loss is loss! Life as we know it will never be the same.

Unbeknownst to me, God continued to orchestrate time, people, and events to bring about my restoration within His "Grand Design." Three precious couples and my daughter's family were determined that I would not become a "loner" as summer approached. They either visited me in my home or I visited them in theirs. We traveled to various sporting events. The wives seemed to enjoy cooking for me as much as I enjoyed being rescued from a steady diet of frozen TV dinners. We laughed, played, and cried together.

Later in the summer, a church friend invited me to teach a weekly Bible study in a home group in our retirement community. God used this study with an informal atmosphere and Christian fellowship to further my healing process. It helped me overcome the anger and bitterness that I had felt since Nita's passing. Several in this group had also lost loved ones. Listening and sharing similar emotions brought a closeness to this group that provided healing to others, including myself. It reminded me of an old adage I had discovered on that first mission trip to Venezuela: As we go forth and minister, so are we ministered unto. I discovered again how reading His Word will always thaw the heart and allow God back in.

Then another amazing event happened. In September, a dear couple from Houston called and insisted that I join them in Oklahoma on a three-day Motorhome trip where I stayed in a nearby motel. I participated in all the activities with them and the group. What fun it was, meeting and discovering that two-thirds of these people lived in my retirement community. Amazing how God works! I had driven out of state just to meet my neighbors! Other invitations and events would soon follow. I sincerely believe that God used my old friends to introduce me to new friends, connecting me to additional streams of support. I was surprised to find that most members of the home study group and new motorhome friends attended the same Sunday school class at my local church. So, I joined that Sunday School class. This provided a continual study and social outlet. Reflecting back, I'm amazed at how God was healing my grief gradually, bringing restoration.

While traveling to my son's home in early November, I was driving in a forested East Texas area. I lost the sports station that I was listening to. So, I started searching for another station. The only program I found was a Christian radio station that was interviewing Gerald Sittser. He was an associate professor of religion at Whitworth College in Spokane, Washington, who had a theology degree from Fuller Seminary. They were talking about how he, his wife, his mother, and three children had driven to an Indian reservation on a mission trip one weekend and were returning home that night. A drunk driver, returning to the reservation, ran into their car. The accident killed his wife, mother, and one daughter. He later wrote about his grief experience in *A Grace Disguised—How the Soul Grows Through Loss.* This interview was amazing! It was as if his words were speaking to me personally and that we were sharing our losses. As this interview ended, I lost the signal to this radio station. During that time, I managed to jot down his website for ordering his book.

I found that discovering the interview on the radio station was a God moment, a divine appointment. Further proof of how God works to orchestrate time, people, and events to bring about His will on earth! To be traveling in a car, at that precise moment, to receive only one radio station's signal and hear what you need to hear! WOW! Yes, that is GOD working on our behalf! Not circumstance. Not destiny. Not coincidence—but God! Amazing love! Amazing grace!

Returning home, I began the arduous task of sorting through Nita's belongings. I also began reading Sittser's book. A few days later, I sifted through hundreds of Christmas cards that my wife had saved over the years. A card was uncovered that was sent to us around Christmas 2006. It was from a widow that we knew previously in the East Texas area.

While looking at the picture of Sue taken with her children, Shannon and Bumper, I began to reflect on our association. Until they relocated, her husband Ed had worked at the bank where I did business. We all attended the same local church and Sunday school class. Our families would also fellowship together through various community events since our children were about the same age. Later, I had refereed football games with Ed for five years. He had a great sense of humor, so our times together were always fun and full of laughter. Soon afterward, however, he died of cancer in his early 40s. His wife, Sue, later started a chapter of Women's Aglow Fellowship in Groveton, an interdenominational group for women similar to our Full Gospel Business Men's Fellowship that I helped charter in East Texas. She spoke at one of our meetings. I had spoken at the ladies' fellowship on two different occasions during the mid-eighties. While traveling through our area, Sue had visited my wife and me on several occasions. I realized that we had not heard from our friend since receiving this Christmas card in 2006. The card also stated that she had spent a lot of time at IHOP in Kansas City, Missouri. For some reason, I could not throw that card away. Laying it aside, I looked at it again a few days later. A desire to contact her arose within me. I wanted to tell her that Nita had died. I tried to contact her at her old address without any result.

While spending Thanksgiving with De'Anne, she shared in my desire to communicate with this former friend. De'Anne found Sue's sons' Facebook page and inquired as to where his mom had relocated. He hadn't used his Facebook page for a year and was about to close it, but something told him to check that account before he did. He saw De'Anne's message asking where his mom was, and he was only too happy to share her cell phone number. Was this a mere coincidence or another God incident?

I discovered that Sue was still living in the same area. Upon returning home, I called and informed her of my wife's passing. She was consoling and thanked me for letting her know. We shared laughable memories and our grief together since we both had lost our spouses to cancer. I knew that she had remarried but learned that her second husband had also died of Alzheimer's 11 years earlier.

Continuing my grief journey. Sittser wrote a **key statement** that changed my perspective on the grief process. He stated:

> "The risk of further loss, therefore, poses a dilemma. The problem of choosing to love again, is that the choice to love means living under the constant threat of further loss. But the problem of choosing not to love is that the choice to turn from love means imperiling the life of the soul, for the soul thrives in an environment of love. Soul-full people love; soul-less people do not. If people want their souls to grow through loss, whatever the loss is, they must eventually decide to love even more deeply than they did before. They must respond to the loss by embracing love with renewed energy and commitment."[1]

Simply put, every person must choose to either continue to grieve or to love again. I had pastored people who had chosen to stay in grief forever. I decided to embrace life and love again!

Confirming that decision, I believe God began to bring restoration to me at a faster pace. My local pastor

EVERY PERSON MUST CHOOSE TO EITHER CONTINUE TO GRIEVE OR TO LOVE AGAIN.

asked me to preach on Sunday night, December 30, 2012, during a special contemplative service. I felt led to give my testimony since it reflected the message of God's love that prevails throughout the Christmas story. As the closing hymn was being sung, a lady came to the altar unexpectedly. With tears streaming down her face, she motioned me to come near. Introducing herself, Leona communicated that she felt the presence of the Holy Spirit during the service. Leona felt instructed to invite me to teach an upcoming prayer study during the Lenten season. I briefly told her that I would be traveling soon and hesitated to commit.

Nevertheless, Leona asked me to call her back after first praying about teaching the study. We exchanged telephone numbers and agreed to talk further the next day. On the way home that night, the experience of giving my testimony brought a feeling of liberation and relief! I could feel the weight of grief being lifted from my shoulders. Though I would continue to experience times of sadness, life began to feel good again!

Spending the next morning praying about this invitation, I suddenly realized that I had never taught a study on prayer. Wow! That's a shocking confession for a retired pastor to make, but it's true. During this time, I remembered "the lady in the street" experience when she approached and asked, "Do you believe in prayer?"

My goodness! Here was another lady in a different setting many years later that God used to get my attention again. The subject was the same—prayer. When I called Leona that afternoon, my response was one of acceptance. I felt confirmation in my spirit and needed to do this study, as much for myself as for others.

I advised her that I would be traveling with a friend to the mountains. There, I would prayerfully decide on the curriculum to use. The study would begin after Ash Wednesday and be part of the church's Lenten preparation for Easter. Leona said that I could use any resource and to call her upon my return. For some reason, I confessed to her my feelings of inadequacy in teaching on prayer since I considered it my greatest spiritual weakness. "I'm undisciplined in prayer," I told her, "and I find it hard to keep focused when praying."

Leona simply replied, "I'm convinced that the Holy Spirit wants you to teach this class. If you're good enough for Him, you're good enough for our class. Call me when you get back. Have fun."

About three days later, I received a request to preach a funeral for a dear friend at a former pastorate in East Texas. Though for a sad reason, the funeral gave me the opportunity to visit with precious friends overnight. They had been such a strong support for me in my time of grief. Returning home the next morning, I decided to call Sue and see her, since she was on the route home. She lived at a Christian encampment in her camper, located close to her former home of many years. Arriving midafternoon and parking, for some reason, I suddenly felt excited like a teenager on his first date. Sue had been gracious to fix homemade soup for us to eat as we visited. That visit lasted three to four hours. She was easy to talk with, as we shared a common history. Surprisingly my testimony about the "lady in the street" asking me the question, "Do you believe in prayer?" blurted out.

Later, I discovered that the question on prayer piqued her interest in me. Though I could not understand why, my emotions were highly nervous and excited during this time. Rising to leave and thanking her for the meal, I told her about traveling to the mountains with my retired pastor friend. Sue said she would pray for us. If I didn't mind, she would mail me a book she wanted me to read.

"That would be great," I said.

As I rose to leave, Sue stood to participate in our goodbye hug by turning her head and laying it upon my chest. It felt right to lightly kiss her on top of her head as we finished hugging. Returning to the car and waving as I drove off, a sense of peace enveloped me that I had not felt for a long time.

The trip to the New Mexico mountains was spiritually and physically refreshing. We nearly froze in my friend's hideaway trailer when the weather turned frigid with single-digit temperatures and snow! It was, however, a wonderful time of fellowship and revitalization. During this time, the Spirit of God confirmed what prayer study to teach.

The study deepened my understanding of prayer. During this time, I also began meeting with the local church's weekly intercessory prayer group. Led by their worship leader, this small group was interdenominational. It became very instrumental in my healing, restorative process and deepened my growth in prayer.

My new-found lady friend and I continued to correspond and talk upon returning from the New Mexico trip. The depth of her understanding and her spiritual wisdom was amazing. She related several experiences from IHOP. We had a good laugh whenever I told her that when I read the Christmas card where she referred to IHOP, I thought it meant that she had been working at the International House of Pancakes. Instead, she had been an active intercessor at the International House of Prayer. Sue indicated that she was coming to the Weatherford area to see a friend from Women's Aglow. The thought occurred to me that I should invite her to come to this special Thursday contemplative worship service. She agreed, so I arranged a motel room for her.

She also attended my prayer study the next day before leaving to stay with her friends in Weatherford over the weekend. They invited me for supper that weekend as we continued to spend quality time together. It was becoming more obvious to me how her spiritual giftings complemented mine in a way that I had not known before.

During this time, she invited me to join her in Kansas City the next month to attend an upcoming "Passion for Jesus" Conference at the International House of Prayer. This conference would be held during the time she attended IHOP prayer sessions and visited friends. I told her I would think about it and call her in a few days with my decision. A serious time of inner reflection occurred during the next few days as I focused on two primary thoughts. *First, was I ready to begin a serious relationship with this lady?* If I was, I definitely needed to find out what IHOP was all about. *Secondly, it seemed that God was wooing me to continue deepening my understanding of prayer.* Continuing to be a "God chaser" since my Venezuelan journeys, I remained open to experience the Holy Spirit in ways unknown to me. Also, I maintained a deep desire to return to foreign missions where signs, wonders, and miracles manifest. Confirming to my lady friend that I would attend the conference, she offered to register me for the event and drive me to and from the airport.

Attending this three-day conference became another "benchmark of faith" for me as I heard the old Gospel story told in a new and different way. I heard the founder of IHOP start a presentation with the question, "Can you look at yourself in a mirror and shout, 'I am God's favorite son or favorite daughter'?"

My interest awoke immediately! I didn't feel that I was God's favorite son; in fact, I didn't know that God had favorites. But this

Scripture opened up to me in a new way as I read, *"... and have put on the new self, which is being renewed in knowledge after the image of its creator."*[2] If someone asked me what I did before retirement, I confess that I often defined myself by the positions I held, by the promotions attained in the corporate world, and by how large the churches had been that I served. To start defining myself from a spiritual identity was a life-altering transformation.

Connecting dots as the speaker continued, he was answering questions raised by me years ago when I asked, "Why did God love me so much as to send the 'lady in the street,' and more recently, 'the lady asking me to lead a prayer study?'"

Yes, we are created in the image of God and in His love which pursues us. I realized once again that God desired to be in an abiding relationship with us. As the speaker continued, I remembered reading key points in his book:

> "The glory of knowing I am pursued by a God who deeply desires me, even in my weakness, is awesome knowledge."[3]

This knowledge gives me **Hope Beyond**! I read further:

> "I can be confident in the fact that God loves me in my immaturity, and in my immaturity, I returned my love back to him. Along with that, because I am loved; and I am a lover of God. I am successful in my humanity as a person during my time on earth. My primary success is because of that one spiritual principle and fact: I am loved, and I am a lover of God. No matter what else happens, I am already successful because I have received His free love and have become a follower of Jesus."[4]

A very unusual spiritual experience happened when I went forward for prayer at the close of the midafternoon service. Standing for at least ten minutes at the altar, waiting for prayer, I was about to return to my seat when a young man approached me. He said nothing as he came near, other than praying in his prayer language. When he laid hands on my shoulders, I immediately began shaking all over. I began to cry and groan uncontrollably. Someone would later tell me that I was "travailing in the Spirit." This continued for ten to fifteen minutes as he began to shout, "Release him, release him!"

I could hardly stand under the weight of the presence of God as I continued to shake, cry, and groan uncontrollably. The young man paused, then walked away. As he departed, my shaking quit, as immediately as it had begun. Continuing to relax for only a minute or so, I looked up and saw the young man approaching again. This "travailing experience" started once more when he laid hands on me again. Lasting for another ten minutes, he departed. I never saw him again. Feeling emotionally and spiritually exhausted, I could barely walk back to where I had been sitting.

Bishop Nathan Strom wrote:

> "Travail in the Greek is the word, *odino*, which is understood with the pangs of childbirth. Travailing is birthing something new through the Spirit …The thing being birthed through the Spirit will always be that which God desires."[5]

I believe by faith that this experience was manifested by God's love through the power of His Holy Spirit. I was being released to RECEIVE:

"Cast your burdens on the Lord [release it] and He will sustain and uphold you. He will never allow the righteous to be shaken [slip, fall, fail]."[6]

"And now I commend you to God [placing you in His protective, loving care] and [I commend you] to the word of His grace [the counsel and promises of His unmerited favor]. His grace is able to build you up and to give you the [rightful] inheritance among all those who are sanctified [that is, among those who are set apart for God's purpose—all believers]."[7]

This spiritual intercession was birthing a new season of transformation with Him. Given at this particular time, this manifestation encouraged my continuing spiritual journey of repentance, redemption, and restoration. Prophetic words received during this conference furthered this understanding.

Saying our goodbyes, I returned home to Texas.

Having participated in this conference brought new perspectives and a deeper understanding of prayer. God was beckoning me to a new vista of **Hope Beyond.**

ENDNOTES

1. Taken from *A Grace Disguised* by Gerald L Sittser, p.165.
2. Colossians 3:10 ESV.
3. *The Pleasures of Loving God* by Mike Bickel, pg. 3.
4. *The Pleasures of Loving God* by Mike Bickel, pg. 15.
5. *Travailing; A Work of Intercession and the Spirit* by Bishop Nathan C. Strom.
6. Psalm 55:22 AMP.
7. Acts 20:32 AMP.

CHAPTER 19

NEW
EXCITEMENT

Experiencing a sense of excitement that I couldn't explain at that moment, the return flight home seemed much quicker. My thought process was consumed with a new spiritual awakening. It reminded me of years ago when I returned from that first Venezuelan mission experience, but under much different circumstances. The similarity was knowing in my heart that God was wooing me to know Him in a way much deeper than before. I couldn't help but ask, "Why now, Lord?"

People always told me that a pastor never retires, but until recently, I had been more retired than active in the church. Was this a continual working of my salvation? The Apostle Paul referred to this in his letter to the Philippians when he wrote: *"... continue to work out your salvation with fear and trembling, for it is God who works in you to will and to act according to his good purpose."*[1]

Was this a blessing of God's love just for me, or was this a blessing received somehow to be a blessing to others, or was it both?

One thing I felt certain about was my previous decision to live and not continue to grieve. Our physical, emotional, and spiritual well-being thrive better in an environment of love. When John wrote his beloved friend, Gaius, he remarked: *"Beloved friend, I pray that you are prospering in every way and that you continually enjoy good health, just as your soul is prospering.*[2]

Spending more time with Sue had also convinced me that she was well worth the "risk to love again." It was amazing to remember how our previous lives had often crossed as well as the familiarity of our children with both families. De'Anne and her husband Michael's spiritual insight would be welcomed, as I planned to share with them what had happened at IHOP before returning home.

Upon Sue's return from Kansas City to Texas, I proposed. She accepted.

We both had mutually agreed and believed that God had brought us together, complementing each other's spiritual giftings. Besides giving us a deep and abiding love for each other, we felt that He had a ministry purpose for us after our season of adjustment passed. Agreeing that a long courtship was not necessary at our age, we were married in a small, family ceremony on June 22, 2013, along with a few endearing friends in attendance. De'Anne later confirmed our decision. She related to me that she and my granddaughter had been praying for me to marry a Christian lady who would complement our spiritual gifting together. During this process, the Lord had also given

De'Anne a dream that whenever I met this woman, we would be married in a short time.

Sometimes our willingness to be open for spiritual change and transformation and adapt to new personal relationships comes face-to-face with reality. I did not realize how set in his ways and habits a 73-year-old man could become after living with one person for over 50 years and being a pastor for over 25 years. Sue was 67 years old and had become very independent while living alone for over 12 years. Like all newlyweds, a time of discovery began with one another. This season furthered my understanding of intercessory prayer daily.

SOMETIMES OUR WILLINGNESS TO BE OPEN FOR SPIRITUAL CHANGE AND TRANSFORMATION AND ADAPT TO NEW PERSONAL RELATIONSHIPS COMES FACE-TO-FACE WITH REALITY.

In the early fall, a dear friend who lived in the community where I had last served invited us to a football game for the weekend. This friend also held a reception introducing Sue to all my friends. It was a wonderful time of celebration and reunion.

In early November, five months after we were married, we made a trip to Southeast Texas, close to the Louisiana border, where Sue's three brothers lived near each other. We stopped over briefly for her annual mammogram checkup near where her daughter lived. The doctor was not pleased with the results. An appointment was made to return the next day. He desired more time to study her mammogram. There is a common and natural reaction of worry and fear whenever a person is told that they might have the "big C." We prayed together that night in the motel until we gained a sense of peace.

Sue asked me, "Did you hear anything during the prayer?"

I responded, "I believe I saw the phrase, 'This is only a hiccup.'"

That may not have been as comforting to her as it was to me. I had been remembering the long, painful suffering that my wife had gone through. For me, "hiccup" meant that we might receive a positive diagnosis while hoping for a negative one; but it would be over a short duration, and her healing would occur. She did receive a positive diagnosis the next day, but with wonderful news! The tumor was in a very early stage. We returned to the car and sat in silence for a few moments. Looking up at me with tears in her eyes, she calmly said, "I'll agree to an annulment or divorce so you won't have to go through this again."

Quickly responding to her, I stated, "There's no way I would ever abandon you to face this by yourself. Besides, this is only a hiccup. Hiccups go away in a brief time."

We continued on the journey to see her brothers.

Returning home, Sue wanted a joyous holiday season. She would seek medical treatment in the New Year. Meanwhile, many prayers were lifted to the Lord for Sue's healing. Still planning ahead, she contacted her dear friend in Weatherford, whose husband was a doctor. She had already experienced a malignancy three years prior. They introduced us to a family surgeon and oncologist in the Fort Worth Metroplex. After a series of appointments, Sue was scheduled for surgery in April. We both believed that God was walking beside her and directing our journey with divine appointments all along the way. Having previously made a similar journey, it was easier for me to advise

Sue on a radiologist and other needed medical personnel. We were as prepared as anyone could be for what might lay ahead. Her surgery was successful and not invasive as all lymph nodes were clear. Radiation followed. Prayers were answered for her healing! Praise God! It was only a hiccup!

Summer was upon us. After weeks of radiation, we were ready to travel and change the scenery. Traveling to meet her extended family at a July 4th celebration in North Dakota was enjoyable. Feelings of kinship arose through their warmth and acceptance of me as a new family member. We enjoyed stopovers in Branson and with her friends at IHOP. Our summer was filled with delightful and relaxing enjoyment.

A call awaited me to return to the community where I had last served to lead a prayer service. This service would begin an emphasis on prayer over nightly meetings the following week. Was it coincidence, or was God orchestrating time, people, and events once again to bring my attention deeper into prayer? Since giving my testimony at the local church where I lived in retirement, I had only been asked to do two programs. Both programs were about prayer. A significant development happened at this time before returning home. We discovered that a house of prayer had begun operation in the community since I had retired and relocated. We were introduced the next day to their leadership before returning home.

Every time we visited Sue's brothers in Southeast Texas, we deviated our route to visit this house of prayer. We became very familiar with its operation and fell in love with the like-minded people of prayer there. It was also much closer than driving to IHOP in Kansas City and gave me opportunities to see old friends again.

Though we did not yet know it, change was on the horizon as we continued our adventure of *Hope Beyond.*

ENDNOTES
1. Philippians 2:12b-13.
2. 3 John 2 TPT.

CHAPTER 20

FEAST AND DRINK

ue and I had held the prophetic word loosely that she was given after our marriage ceremony from one of my dear friends, Deborah, who boldly declared:

"The Lord told me that you guys will be moving back. He didn't say when."

Sue responded with laughter, then said, "We'll see."

With a twinkle in her eye, Deborah retorted, "Oh, Oh, Oh! You will!"

Relocating was certainly not on our radar at the time we got married. A year later, however, I was hearing and sensing the call of God. This would overcome my objections to giving up my perfect retirement setting. One purpose of our marriage was to be obedient to the leading of the Holy Spirit. We both desired to "run the race that God set before us" during our remaining years. Running this race together would be better than separate.

"How priceless is your unfailing love! Both high and low among men find refuge in the shadow of your wings. They feast on the abundance of your house; you give them drink from your river of delights. For with you is the fountain of life; in your light we see light. Continue your love to those who know you, your righteousness to the upright in heart."[1]

We settled in a pleasant place. It was a rural setting where houses weren't stacked upon each other. The location was only ten minutes away from everything we needed. Any relocation causes a season of adjusting to everything that is new and different.

We were obedient to the call of moving to volunteer our services in this house of prayer without any ulterior motives. Originally, we were the only "gray hairs" among young families. It was pure delight being "young again" and associating with like-minded spiritual people! The ministry's leadership accepted and included us in this prayer work. We gave of our services whenever asked and became faithful in our attendance, worship, and support.

Their worship meetings didn't interfere with our worshiping on Sunday mornings at the church I had previously served. We enjoyed having fellowship with old friends. Occasional substitute teaching for a Sunday school class filled a void that I enjoyed.

The old adage, "Time passes quickly when you're having fun," certainly applied to this season of our lives. It was early February 2017, and in less than four months, we would celebrate two years in our new location and our fourth wedding anniversary.

I received a phone call that brisk morning from Elizabeth, a friend from our Sunday school class. Elizabeth began telling me about her recent prayer experience. Explaining that she had always wanted to host a Bible study in her home, she believed that the Lord instructed her that the time was now. Elizabeth then related how she asked Him for guidance on who would teach the class, then mentioned some names to Him for clarification.

"Guess who God highlighted?" she said.

"I'm afraid to answer," I replied.

As we laughed together, my immediate reaction was to thank her for her confidence while I thought to myself, *not another Bible study!*

Though there were many exceptions to the norm, one of my major disappointments in ministry had been watching Christians participate in studies and never seem to mature or make transformational changes. In my opinion, some would sit like a sponge, listen to a lecture, be spoon-fed, and then depart. After attending Sunday church, it seemed that many felt good about having accomplished their weekly religious obligations. As far as I could determine, no real differences were apparent in their lives.

As the Apostle Paul once described,

> *"Anyone who lives on milk, being still an infant, is not acquainted with the teaching about righteousness. But solid food is for the mature, who by constant use have trained themselves to distinguish good from evil."*[2]

My desire was simply to teach "solid food," resulting in transformational change.

I ended the conversation by thanking Elizabeth again for this invitation and her willingness to be the host. I told her that I would pray about it and give her my answer in a couple of days. She agreed to my request. The conversation ended.

Arising from my chair, I found Sue on the porch. I told her about the conversation. Her only remark was, "Are you going to do it?"

"I really don't know," I replied.

As Sue retired that evening and we said our goodnights, I told her that I would stay up for a while, praying. I would try to discern what the Lord wanted me to do; otherwise, I would probably say no. My thoughts were immediately directed to how the Lord had brought women to refocus and guide my spiritual journey since the "lady in the street" experience. I did feel humbled that Elizabeth had called me in obedience to the Lord. Having done all in preparing my heart, mind, and spirit to receive what word the Lord might offer me this night, I sat quietly.

I was not disappointed. A clear, vivid impression soon entered my mind causing me to repent of my previous thoughts. God's presence was strong. He whispered, "I'm so glad to know, Ferel, that you finally got it together."

Instantly, I felt His words were a rebuke. Bowing my head and kneeling, I sensed my guilt and shame. With tears in my eyes, I confessed, "Sorry, Lord, please forgive me. Lord, please help me! You know my heart. My desire is for a study that goes beyond the surface and touches the hem of Your garment. A study that will move people into a more intimate and personal relationship with Your Son, Jesus. Help me, Lord, that any study I teach will be directed by Your Holy Spirit. Help me prayerfully to provide a setting where each participant will be open to You. A place where each will mature in their giftings. Send those who are willing to stretch and grow their spiritual lives with integrity and thorough self-examination. Help me, Lord, to put aside my usual preparation with commentaries and other narratives. Forgive me, Lord, that I've often prepared in my own effort. I'm determined with Your help, Lord, to do this study strictly with Your guidance through the Holy Spirit, from beginning to end—in Jesus' name, amen."

Needless to say, I agreed to teach this study. It would begin in mid-September. God granted every request from my prayer that night. It was the beginning of a new, miraculous, and wonderful experience as I would receive a "download" from the Holy Spirit for each session. My hand would write on paper as quickly as it could. I was amazed how the Holy Spirit would also place impressions in my mind that would lead me to other resources.

As I write these words today, I felt led to begin this chapter with verses from Psalm 36. God continues to connect dots in my spiritual journey and re-emphasize that there is a purpose to every season. Though we know that all have sinned and come short of the glory of God, how priceless is God's unfailing love! Even as a pastor, I confess that I did not feel fulfillment in my spiritual stature of maturity. I yearned for more as I continued in a quest to uncover His truth. Each person who joined this class also had a yearning for more of Him, to grow in intimacy with Him, and to totally recommit their lives to Him. They desired to partner with Him in bringing His kingdom to earth. Several shared that they had secret desires that had not been satisfied in serving Him. As I reread the verses of Psalm 36:7-10, I was learning to feast in the abundance of His house and to drink in His river of delights that result in discovering the fountain of life: *"For with you is the fountain of life; in your light we see light."*[3]

God was unveiling a "fountain of life" in Him that was engaging, gripping, absorbing, and involving. A person's spiritual journey doesn't have to be boring, stale, wearisome, or uninteresting. It can be dynamic, not static.

My home study preparation for the final fall session was unusual and freely given by God's Holy Spirit. I believe it blessed each class member, as well as me. Walking one morning with nothing specific on my mind, I offered a short declaration of thanksgiving and praise to the Lord. God had met my prayer request for the class. Continuing to walk in silence, I suddenly saw a vision of a class member face-to-face. Several scenes followed. Then I began to receive a download [a prophetic message of healing] that I was to give this person in private. This experience ended as fast as it had begun. I had received prophetic messages for people before, but I had never received a vision and message quite like this one.

Usually, I lose a prophetic message if I don't give it promptly. I hurried home to write it down. However, this message was different as it stayed vividly in my mind and burned within my spirit. Upon arriving home, I grabbed a tablet and went to my patio, where I could sit quietly. I wrote what had happened. As I finished writing this down, another class member's name appeared. A prophetic message was given for them also. Two and one-half hours later, the Lord had given me prophetic messages for half of the class. The next morning, on my patio, God gave me prophetic messages for the others.

I now realize that each message was to help each class member "feast in the abundance of His house and drink in His river of delights,"[4] which results in discovering their fountain of life in Him. Offering that opportunity to every person is God's desire.

Though the home study group was several years ago, while praying today, I received further understanding. This home group formed another layer of spiritual foundation that God desired me to possess as I grow in spiritual understanding and maturity. Receiving revelation, knowledge, and guidance from Him through the Holy Spirit is ongoing. It's learning to *"feast on the abundance of your house; you give them drink from your river of delights. For with you is the fountain of life; in your light we see light."[5]* It's about growing in our understanding of intimacy and personal relationship with Him. Jesus said, *"Live in me. Make your home in me just as I do in you."[6]* This becomes a dynamic relationship that is constant and as real as two friends who talk with each other daily.

What a gift of God's unfailing love to enjoy forever! Whether you're a believer or a non-believer, I declare unto you in this moment: "God has unfailing love for you! He desires that you discover your fountain of life in Him!" In doing so, this discovery will usher forth your **Hope Beyond!**

ENDNOTES

1. Psalm 36:7-10.
2. Hebrews 5:13-14.
3. Psalm 36:9.
4. Psalm 36:8.
5. Psalm 36:8-9.
6. John 15:4a MSG.

GOD HAS UNFAILING LOVE
FOR YOU! HE DESIRES
THAT YOU DISCOVER YOUR
FOUNTAIN OF LIFE IN HIM!

CHAPTER 21

ᗞISCOVERING ᕼIS ᖴOUNTAIN OF ᒪIFE

For days I had hummed a familiar song that I often enjoy singing, entitled "King of My Heart" by Sarah & John Mark McMillan.[1] If you have never heard it, go to YouTube and look up the performance by Kutlass.[2] The words epitomized the continuance of feasting on the abundance of our heavenly Father's house and drinking from His river of life that enabled us to discover His fountain of life—"the fountain I drink from." For in God's light, we see light.

The home Bible study group continued for another three-month session. In the meantime, I had previously read three of the writings of Jonathan Cahn. His *Book of Mysteries* unlocked many biblical truths that I had often overlooked. Daily readings became a seeking process of receiving new revelation and connecting the dots of understanding for my personal journey. God used Cahn's proficiency in the Hebrew language to connect many truths with the New Testament. This process helped me understand how methodical God had been throughout the generations in bringing His kingdom to earth. In retrospect, I continue to be amazed at how subtly God works in the lives of those who seek Him.

For example, it was late February 2018. I walked into the room where Sue was watching a biblical program on TV. To my amazement, Jonathan Cahn was the guest. He was giving further insight into his *Book of Mysteries*. What my inner spirit reacted to, however, was an advertisement during the program that spoke about his upcoming fall tour to Israel. Suddenly, it was as if my entire being knew that I was to make this trip. Hurriedly, I jotted down the contact number that flashed across the screen. When the program was over, I asked Sue, "Would you like to make a trip to Israel with me?"

Taken by surprise, she replied, "Let's pray about it."

Before the week was over, Sue had decided to stay; but agreed that I should go. I hesitated to leave her, but she urged me to do so.

I called the following Monday, paid my deposit, and was told that I was fortunate to make this tour. There were only two single spaces left to fill. That was my confirmation to go.

Was it a mere coincidence that I walked into the room where my wife was watching this television program?

Was it a mere coincidence that I began to watch also?

No, it was not a coincidence that sensitized my ears to hear. It was the Holy Spirit.

I entered that room for another purpose. As my attention turned to the television, I suddenly knew that whatever was being said,

I needed to hear. Yes, God's orchestration of circumstances was right on time! Yet, it's still our choice to pursue the journey with Him or not. My experience was not as dramatic as the burning bush that God had prepared for Moses, but it was significant to me. Both experiences are similar in that we have the freedom to choose. It is up to the individual involved whether we investigate what we see and hear or ignore it completely.

Six weeks before I left for Israel, Sue was surprised to receive a call from Esther, a friend in nearby East Texas. She had not seen or talked to her for several years. Esther was coming to our area and wanted to visit with us for a couple of days. Sue is always hospitable, generous, and has an open-door policy to everyone—especially family, spiritual confidants, and prayer partners.

After Esther's arrival, one afternoon, as we three were sharing prayer time together, Esther turned to me and began giving a prophetic word. This word became so significant in the unfolding of both my personal and spiritual journey in the days ahead. She prophesied:

> "... God sees your heart ... God is letting you have the availability to stand at His door ... Say yes to receive His gift ... It's your choice to open the door ... If you open the door, He will show you the fullness of what He wants you to see and receive. It will be an impartation from Him to you, so you will be able to accomplish your deepest desires with His anointing ... to minister to people with signs, wonders, and miracles following ... Will it be immediate? I don't know! It will be determined by developing a deeper relationship with Him in your secret place. The time is now."

WOW! AMAZING! I'm eager to accept God's invitation to receive all that He has prepared for me. To be honest, at this moment, I'm was not sure what that entails, but I was open and full of anticipation and excitement!

Being the recipient of these words was very humbling. I remembered listening to an evangelist once say that receiving prophetic words does not guarantee that they will come to pass. This becomes a process of surrendering to Him. Then the seeker sets aside time to pray, fast, and read God's Word. When we receive a word, we are to continue growing in intimacy and maturity until God has given us the fullness of what He wants us to see and receive.

My deepest desire has been to preach, on every occasion, as the Apostle Paul described;

"My message and my preaching were not with wise and persuasive words, but with a demonstration of the Spirit's power, so that your faith might not rest on men's wisdom, but on God's power."[3]

This prophetic message, received from Esther, validated the psalmist's words: *"How priceless is your unfailing love ... feast on the abundance of your house; you give them drink from your river of delights. For with you is the fountain of life; in your light we see light."[4]*

Experiences like this reinforce my faith, increase my obedience to follow Him, and confirm the presence of the living God who works in me through the power of His Holy Spirit. It further elevates my boldness, courage, commitment, and undying love for Jesus, the Lord of lords.

"As it is written: no eye has seen, no ear has heard, no mind has conceived what God has prepared for those who love him—but God has revealed it to us by his Spirit."[5]

Yes, *"how priceless is the unfailing love of God"* who offers His love to every person to discover His own *"fountain of life"* flowing within ... as well as His **Hope Beyond!**

ENDNOTES

1. *King of My Heart* by Sarah & John Mark McMillan. © 2015 Meaux Jeaux Music (SESAC) Raucous Ruckus Publishing (SESAC) (adm. at CapitolCMGPublishing.com) / Sarah McMillan Publishing (SESAC) (adm. at WatershedMusicPublishing.com). All Rights Reserved. Used by Permission.
2. https://www.youtube.com/watch?v=R2eNsXwlLvo.
3. 1 Corinthians 2:4-5.
4. Psalm 36:7-10.
5. 1 Corinthians 2:9-10a.

RECEIVING PROPHETIC WORDS DOES
NOT GUARANTEE THEY WILL COME
TO PASS. THERE IS A PROCESS OF
SURRENDERING TO GOD—PRAYING,
FASTING, READING HIS WORD—GROWING
IN INTIMACY AND MATURITY UNTIL GOD
HAS GIVEN THE FULLNESS OF WHAT
HE WANTS US TO SEE AND RECEIVE.

CHAPTER 22

To Walk Where Jesus Walked

Thirty-one days after receiving the prophetic word from Esther, as Sue and I were ending our morning prayer session, she grew suddenly quiet, straightened up, and began to relate what she was "seeing" in a vision.

"Ferel," she said, "I see you standing by yourself with a heavenly presence placing a poncho over your head. The poncho is made of hemp fiber which is light but very strong."

Quickly, the interpretation came, as she continued, "The poncho is a covering of protection, guidance, and provision of whatever will be needed during the upcoming trip to Israel."

Hearing these words made me feel humble, overwhelmed by God's love. Coming from Sue was a double blessing! How precious is our heavenly Father's unfailing love for His children!

My mind recalled my trip to Venezuela thirty-five years earlier, where I experienced that "covering." Such was unknown to me then but truly welcomed.

Thank God for wonderful daughters willing to help their dads. I traveled to DeAnne's house the night before departure, and she drove me to the Dallas-Fort Worth International Airport the next morning. Saying goodbyes to Sue and De'Anne, excitement grew within me as I walked to the gate for departure to Kennedy International in New York. The four-hour layover would be helpful for possible schedule delays and for checking in for departure to a foreign country.

It didn't take long for this Texas boy to wish for the uncrowded spaces he was accustomed to as I navigated through Kennedy International. It was like descending into a sea of people rushing to and fro in all directions. I walked to the side of the corridor where I could stand without being run over. It was a maze trying to read all the signs where the arrows were pointing to know which tram to ride. Only a minute or two had passed when suddenly a nice gentleman walked up to me and said, "You look confused. Can I help you?"

"You sure can," I replied. "Thank you."

Within 60 seconds, he had directed me to where I needed to go. Mumbling under my breath as I merged into the sea of people, I simply said, "Thank you, Lord, for your covering that provides whatever I need, whenever I need it."

The circumstances were similar to my Venezuela trip except with a lot more people. What fun it is to travel with the Holy Spirit. Riding trams is an experience in itself, especially when you have carry-on luggage, people standing elbow to elbow, and a loudspeaker barking at you to get ready to depart at the next stop.

This environment creates a noise level that makes it very difficult for people like me who depend on a hearing aid. I was fortunate to depart at the wrong place only once, and I soon discovered it was the wrong terminal. Retracing my steps and reentering the tram once again, I remembered the words of Sue, who often said, "How fun it is to get lost, so you can find yourself again."

Counting the time change, I realized that I had been up fourteen hours when the tour group finally boarded the flight to Israel around 8:00 pm. The plane would arrive in Tel Aviv, Israel, around 12:00 noon, which is 5:00 am New York time. There is a seven-hour time difference between New York and Israel. My enthusiasm for having a window seat and flying in a new plane quickly waned. This plane had wonderful amenities, but space behind first-class seats was very limited. I had to crawl over the two occupants next to me while asking the people in the row in front of me to raise their seatbacks, just so I wouldn't knock their heads off. When seated next to the window, even moving my head to look out was enough to knock my cap off. Needless to say, very little sleep occurred during that twelve-hour journey.

Following arrival at Ben Gurion Airport near Tel Aviv and walking to our designated tour meeting place, I began to sense a change in the spiritual environment. This shift in the atmosphere restored my physical energy, excitement, and expectation. I thought, *Was this in my mind?*

Nearly everyone on the bus commented that they had sensed it too! I knew that we were walking on Holy Ground! It brought to mind one of my favorite songs. I began to hum to myself as I walked: *"We are standing on holy ground, and I know that there are angels all around. Let us praise Jesus now; we are standing in His presence on holy ground."*[1]

We were greeted graciously by our host and given colored ID badges which reflected our assigned bus. It was around 2:30 pm as we departed Ben Gurion Airport driving along the Mediterranean shores. Soon we arrived at the ancient city of Jappa, spelled Joppa today. The tour guide began by telling us what Tel Aviv meant in Hebrew. This definition seems to define much of Israel. "Tel" in Hebrew means "old." Complex Hebrew states that "Tel" is an archaeological feature common to Israel, inhabited by people for thousands of years. "Tel" is a mound underneath, which lay on the ruins of previous settlements. "Aviv" means "spring" and represents a rebirth of the nation in a place where it had previously settled. It's the "old" becoming "new," and that's a relevant definition for Israel today. Everywhere we went, we saw uncovered ruins with new structures being built around them and above them. The old culture met with modern culture. It was a beautiful sight to behold.

The part of Joppa known as "Jappa" was the ancient port city visited by Peter as described in Acts 10. It is a place sacred to Christians. After visiting several historical sites, we departed from the bus and began a short walk up the hill. *I wonder where are we going?* I thought to myself.

Walking to where our guide had stopped at the top of the hill behind shrubbery, I could see a small alleyway between two buildings up ahead. Continuing with the group, we came to a small cobblestone street that was very slick from wear. Being told that this street was between 2,500 and 3,000 years old put me into a state of euphoria! I envisioned people dressed in biblical clothes walking down the streets in conversation amid small carts being pulled by donkeys. People were causing congestion. To walk where Jesus and His disciples walked was overwhelming! What I had read in the Bible was coming to life. As I continued to walk, a new perspective was gained in seeing the actual. The ancient cobblestone street seemed only to be 15 feet wide. Solid three to five-story buildings were on the left. The buildings on the right side of the narrow street had shops with apartments above them displaying small patios overlooking the street. We slowly walked approximately the length of a football field when the small street turned 90° to the left and ended approximately 30 steps in front of us. Amazing!

Our group contained forty-five people. We huddled close together as our guide began to talk. "Look to the closed doorway on the right. Above the door, you will see a plaque with the inscription 'Simon's House.'"

This was the actual house where Simon the tanner had lived. Simon had hosted Peter, the disciple, who had come from nearby Lydda at the request of believers in Joppa, where he raised Tabitha from the dead. Peter remained in Joppa a few more days as a guest at the house of Simon, the tanner. As the guide continued to read Acts 10, I looked above the one-story house. Seeing the flat roof and a medium-sized tree, I visualized where Peter had the vision before meeting the three men, who were sent to Joppa by Cornelius, a Roman captain and believer. Peter would depart the next day with these men to nearby Caesarea, where he spoke at the house of Cornelius. This one event opened the door for all Gentiles, any person not Jewish, to have the opportunity to become believers in the Lord Jesus Christ. God was declaring that every person has special dignity, worth, and uniqueness. God's Son, Jesus, had been sacrificed for the entire world. WOW! To see this and stand right where it happened was absolutely astounding!

On the eighth day of the tour, we drove approximately thirty miles into the countryside outside Jerusalem. Turning down a small, unpaved country road, we weaved slowly around the hills, looking at the landscape. Cresting the top of the small hill, we could see a vast desert on one side contrasted with shrubbery, grassland, and a few trees on the other coming together in the valley below. Departing from the bus in the sunshine, we walked to an open area where we discovered a small tree farm dedicated to land restoration in Israel. We were told that planting a tree on the mountains of the Promised Land helps fulfill Bible prophecy as God blesses those who give life to His land. One tree had been provided for each of us by the tour group. I purchased one more tree to honor Sue. Planting trees was a fun exercise as they led us to the side of the hill that had been lightly cultivated so we could plant trees. My two tree seedlings were planted easily. I then stood on the side of the hill, enjoying the contrasting landscape with a slight breeze blowing on my face. Hearing gunfire toward the desert, we were told that it was a training ground for Israeli soldiers. *Eye-opening,* I thought. The peaceful solitude of the moment had been broken with the stark realization that Israel fights for survival each day. Peaceful tranquility is a gift from God to be treasured.

As the group began walking toward the bus, I noticed that our sunshine had given way to a cloud that had formed toward Jerusalem. As I continued to look, a rainbow suddenly appeared right in front of us. One end came down upon a grove of trees in the valley below the hill where we were walking and had planted the trees. I shouted to the others to look quickly so they could enjoy the moment. I had always wanted to see the end of a rainbow. Today that wish had been granted. God truly blessed us with His rainbow as we had given of our time to bless His land. A miracle! As the buses departed from the tree farm, the rainbow and cloud disappeared as quickly as they had appeared.

Whether it was:

- walking the shores at the Sea of Galilee,
- sitting on the mountain where Jesus taught the Beatitudes,
- walking out of the synagogue in Capernaum to see Peter's house only a short distance down the street,
- ascending Masada,
- discovering the desert blooming with crops, flowers, and fruit trees,
- walking inside the great walls of Jerusalem,
- praying at the Western Wall,
- marveling at the Temple Mount,
- visiting ancient ruins and excavation sites,
- or participating in an inspiring communion service where Jesus was betrayed in the garden of Gethsemane at the Mount of Olives, one thing was certain:

The presence of God, through the Holy Spirit, was constant, real, and overpowering.

His presence was not surprising since God intervenes daily in the restoration of His land and His people. God is preparing for the second coming of His Son, Jesus, the Christ, the Savior for all. To walk where Jesus, His disciples, and the early believers had lived and died was a life-changing experience. For me, it became another "benchmark of faith" that continues to build the substance of faith in my *Hope Beyond.*

185

ENDNOTE

1. *Holy Ground* by Geron Davis. © 1983 Meadowgreen Music Company (Admin. by Capitol CMG Publishing), Songchannel Music (Admin. by Capitol CMG Publishing).

CHAPTER 23

CONNECTING DOTS

The phone rang during the first week of February 2019. I recognized the voice of a pastor friend who invited me to preach during spring break while he was taking a short vacation with family. I eagerly accepted and looked forward to standing in the pulpit again. The unfailing love of my heavenly Father would use my preparation of this message to culminate and clarify thirty-eight years of overlooking His foremost purpose in sending the "lady in the street," who walked boldly up to me and asked, "Ferel, do you believe in prayer?"

When she confronted me, my mind had remembered the seminary professor who told me that prayer was a figment of my imagination. Though it had been transformational and life-changing to witness the events that followed, I had focused more on the dramatic—the signs, wonders, and miracles—than I did on God's question. I had overlooked the essence and depth of what God the Father was attempting to communicate.

The heart of the matter was simply, "Ferel, do you believe in prayer?"

Isn't this the essence and heart of being in a personal and intimate relationship with Him that leads to fruitful ministry? Jesus said, *"I am the vine; you are the branches. Whoever abides in me and I in him, he it is that bears much fruit, for apart from me you can do nothing."*[1]

God's question was again like a sword that cut deep within my spirit. My confession was "tragic" because I did not have an intimate, deep, abiding prayer life until I began experiencing houses of prayer and daily prayer with Sue. Most of my prayers were shallow, containing a wish list. I needed that intimate, personal relationship with Jesus that only comes through an active prayer life. This demands setting aside time to be with Him! In retrospect, I again sought the Lord's forgiveness that this previous shepherd of His flock failed to provide this key understanding for God's people. Far too often, as a pastor, I had witnessed churchgoers who did not have an active prayer life. In my opinion, they didn't understand what it meant to have an intimate personal relationship with the Lord either.

Yes, I can remember times when I was driven to my knees in desperation to God because I could not solve the situation at hand. My type of prayer life reminded me of someone who carried a handkerchief in their pocket for an occasional sneeze. Pull it out when all else fails. Sometimes my desperate prayers and cries for help concluded in further frustration; either I didn't get the answers I desired or the mess I created somehow solved itself. Often, God was merciful and offered His grace to me. Even though I was totally undeserving, my prayers were answered. Did that change my spiritual behavior? More often than not, it didn't.

I would go on my way until the next time. Matthew recorded, *"And after Jesus had dismissed the crowds, he went up on the mountain by himself to pray. When evening came, he was there alone."[2]*

I was always amazed to read how Jesus, the Son of God, set Himself apart to pray daily with His heavenly Father. Suddenly, it dawned on me! If this was important for God's Son to do, how much more necessary it becomes for every follower of Jesus to do the same? My thoughts returned again to the question, "Ferel, do you believe in prayer?"

Suddenly and simply, the pieces of my spiritual journey and understanding from recent seasons began coming into focus. Prayer was the gateway to entering into a personal and intimate relationship with Him. I realized Jesus desired this more than any service that I could offer to Him! I was learning a very valuable lesson that Peter learned when Jesus washed his feet. I must first receive "from Jesus" before I entered into fruitful service "for Him." I must first receive His love before I would know how to love. Paul's words reflect this process, *"For now we see in a mirror dimly, but then face to face. Now I know in part; then I shall know fully, even as I have been fully known."[3]*

The sermon preparation came to a halt! I began reflecting on how the Spirit of the Lord had directed my spiritual journey even without me realizing what was happening. It first began with the home study group in September 2017, ending in May 2018. From the very first lesson, it was about engaging in prayer and intimacy. The Spirit of the Lord had directed me to Psalm 100. This Psalm became a learning key. It provided new understanding of how I was to approach God in prayer. It's wasn't complicated at all! I approached God in prayer in the same manner that I approach

Him in worship, which is to *"Enter His gates with thanksgiving and His courts with praise; give thanks to Him and praise His name."[4]*

Simply stated: I shifted agendas. I quit coming to God with my "wish list" first. Instead, I came to God, first, for His agenda. Having the key to enter into His sanctuary, God then revealed a second principle: *"Who may ascend the hill of the Lord? Who may stand in his holy place? He who has clean hands and a pure heart ..."[5]*

> I SHIFTED AGENDAS. I QUIT COMING TO GOD WITH MY "WISH LIST" FIRST. INSTEAD, I CAME TO GOD, FIRST, FOR HIS AGENDA.

Learning these simple truths changed not only my perspective on how to pray, but also opened the door which led me to a deepening intimate and personal relationship with the Lord. Learning to listen, first, helped me to abide more and more in Him. This approach enabled me to partner with Him in bringing about His kingdom on earth. Apart from Him, we can do nothing. The sermon was preached. New revelation had come in the process!

Continuing to reflect on the spiritual journey the Lord was directing, Sue and I traveled in our small camper during the summer of 2018 to our favorite places to get away from the Texas heat. Upon returning, I remembered how the Holy Spirit had directed Esther to visit us from East Texas and offer me a prophetic word before leaving. The main emphasis was: "Ferel, you are standing at God's door, where God is inviting you to enter." Less than 60 days after her visit, I traveled to Israel and experienced the most inspiring spiritual adventure of my life.

In the summer of 2019, Sue and I would again return to northern Montana, where we attended a family church camp for inspiration, fellowship, and relaxation among friends. After the speaker spoke on Thursday evening, I asked Sue to join me at the altar for prayer, as I felt a leading by the Holy Spirit. The front quickly filled with people standing three deep. We stood there for fifteen minutes at least. Sue wanted to sit back down, but I urged her to stay a few more minutes. I felt at the time that it might be a test to see my commitment and sincerity, for similar waits like this had occurred previously. Within a couple of minutes, one of the pastors on stage walked towards Sue. As he walked within six feet of her, the presence and Spirit of God was so strong that it knocked her backward with great force. She became like a bowling ball knocking over people, including me, like bowling pins. When trying to get up, she found it difficult to stand underneath the weight of God's presence. I retrieved a chair for her to sit in, helping her up. The pastor prayed and prophesied over her, but my hearing aids diminished my hearing. I had no understanding of what he had told her.

He finished, turned to me, and asked, "Do you want prayer also?"

I replied, "Yes!"

He immediately began prophesying over me. His word was revealing and encouraging. After the service, the pastor agreed to meet me the next day to discuss further the interpretation and questions that I had. After visiting the next day for a while, he said to me in closing with a smile on his face, "Though you are a stranger to me, I feel that I know your heart from our conversation. I want you to consider joining our mission team to the Dominican Republic in November of this year."

My heart and spirit leaped for joy as I replied, "You mean you would welcome a pastor from a different denomination to join you?"

"Oh yes," he added, "for we are kingdom builders, not denomination builders."

I told him I would consider it, thanking him for the invitation. Later that afternoon, I told Sue about our conversation. Tears came to my eyes as I again remembered prophetic words given to me by Esther. I believe this pastor's invitation resulted from being behind God's door in our secret place. God was calling me to enjoy one of many aspects of His fullness that He wanted me to receive and see by going on this mission trip. Partnering with Him, I knew that signs, wonders, and miracles would follow.

"Yes," my heart responded.

That night before the worship service began, a lady was seated directly in front of me. I didn't know her and had never met her before. Suddenly and without warning, she turned around and began to prophesy over me. She affirmed what I had heard from the pastor the night before and during our conversation after lunch. Elation overcame me! I knew beyond a shadow of a doubt that I was to accept the invitation to join this mission team going to the Dominican Republic.

God's unfailing love, goodness, and grace are priceless. How methodical God had been in getting me to this time and place! My purpose in sharing this chronological sequence has been to convince you, the reader, that these events happened not by mere coincidence but by the very hand of God. The words of Solomon seem so appropriate at this time. *"In his heart, a man plans his course, but the Lord determines his steps."*[6]

I am not wise or clever enough to have foreplanned the experiences encountered on my spiritual journey. Peter says it much better than me,

"We did not follow cleverly invented stories when we told you about the power and coming of our Lord Jesus Christ."[7]

For me, experiencing a personal and loving God who orchestrates time, people, and events has become the bedrock of **Hope Beyond!**

ENDNOTES

1. John 15:5 ESV.
2. Matthew 14:23 ESV.
3. 1 Corinthians 13:12 ESV.
4. Psalm 100:4.
5. Psalm 24:3-4a.
6. Proverbs 16:9.
7. 2 Peter 1:16.

GOD'S UNFAILING LOVE,
GOODNESS, AND GRACE ARE
PRICELESS. HE ORCHESTRATES
EVENTS IN OUR LIVES BY HIS
LOVING, FAITHFUL HAND.

CHAPTER 24

ONE DESIRE FULFILLED

The husband and wife leading the team to the Dominican Republic in November were also camp directors at the summer camp we were attending. This allowed Sue and me to meet them and discuss participation in the upcoming trip. It was helpful to give them preliminary information that they needed. The director advised that he would be sending further details in late August. I invited Sue to join me on this journey, but she felt I should make this trip by myself.

In March 1984, my mission trip to Venezuela gave me one of my strongest "benchmarks of faith." There I witnessed signs, wonders, and miracles that brought transformation instantly to every person involved. The Holy Bible truly came alive before my eyes. It was "truth" as written. What I had witnessed and testified to in Venezuela was not a figment of my imagination! I departed from home with a "Jesus of the mind" and returned with a "Jesus of the heart."

Often wondering over the years why I didn't see signs, wonders, and miracles on a greater scale than a few places in the United States, I have now concluded that it's because much of the church and seminaries in America have compromised the Word leading to apostasy, embracing false ideologies, and adhering to culture rather than to righteousness and holiness. Many have also removed the power of the Holy Spirit from their teachings and the gifts of the Holy Spirit from their worship. This removal has resulted in many young pastors and church leaders leading their congregations astray. Removing the Holy Spirit denies the very presence of God Himself. God's Holy Spirit is the enabler of transformation that brings hope and unity for His church.

Sue and I continued on our summer journey, praying daily. As our prayer ended one morning, she turned to me and said, "I know how important the trip to Venezuela was to your faith. Be open, however, for fresh moves and new revelation from the Holy Spirit. The trip to the Dominican Republic will be different but just as fulfilling."

We didn't realize at the time how prophetic her words would be, for God had many more surprises in store.

The first surprise and clarifying my purpose in going was when Sue invited four dear friends to our home on October 10, 2019, to pray about this trip. These four friends are very special to us. Both couples are intercessory missionaries who are obedient to God's directives to go and pray all over the USA and the world. We had participated in several prayer sessions and journeys together.

Following supper, we gathered in the den. Coming into His presence with thanksgiving and praise, His presence overcame us. We became silent before Him. Priscilla began to pray, and this prophetic word came forth:

"Ferel, you are to release a prophetic vein that God has created in the ground of the Dominican Republic. It will rise and transform the atmosphere over the nation— then fall back down to the ground as rain. When this happens, God will pour His anointing upon the church, and a great revival will sweep the land. God loves these people and desires that none would perish. He wants His church ready for the second coming of His Son. It is significant that you declare this word everywhere you walk in the DR, even more important than speaking to a large audience."

Her husband, Aquilla, then added, *"God's Holy Spirit will become like a mighty highway being built throughout the land with a gigantic bulldozer that will overcome every obstacle and remove every mountain. This mission will bring much joy to you, for you delight in doing the will of my Father."*

I softly began sobbing when I heard the words that *"much joy and delight come to me in doing the will of my Father."*

How true that is! Then Nathan added further understanding about the word *"delight,"* as found in this scripture: *"I delight to do your will, O my God; your law is within my heart."*[1] Paula and Sue added additional words of protection, encouragement, and understanding about what had been said prophetically. Everyone received a blessing from the Lord's Presence that evening.

Having said our goodbyes, I settled into my favorite recliner, replaying the prophetic words that had been given. Our prayer session together was exhilarating yet sobering! The words of Jesus recorded in John's Gospel had a much deeper and abiding meaning to me now, since I was growing in my understanding of intimacy.

"Jesus said, 'I am the vine; you are the branches. If a man remains in me and I in him, he will bear much fruit; apart from me you can do nothing.'"[2]

As I continued to meditate, the sense of reverent fear of my heavenly Father heightened within me. I realized once again who my Creator was! I define reverent fear not as being afraid of God but taking the proper posture of respect and humility before Him. It is partnering with Him in bringing His will and kingdom to earth. I learned an attitude of surrender by placing myself at His feet. This is a prerequisite for ministry in His name. Spiritual maturity brings the understanding that the servant must always decrease so our Lord will increase, for without Him, we can do nothing.

On the morning of October 31, at 5:30 am, I awakened. Turning over, I received a God dream. The dream is most vivid and descriptive as a vision. I was standing in an open space when a faceless man in white was suddenly standing before me. I knew instinctively that this was a heavenly messenger. His message was clearly understandable without hearing an audible voice. The messenger conveyed that I would meet a pastor in the Dominican Republic that needed healing. He had been grieving for over two years about his son's death. God wanted to heal his broken heart and restore him. God the Father needed him to stop grieving, focus on his love for God, and become the shepherd of the people by living his faith before them. The messenger then gave me the first and middle names of the pastor and his son. He then disappeared just as quickly as he had appeared.

Awaking and rising quickly, I went into the other room to write down the details of this dream. I had never experienced a dream such as this! I was eager to share what had happened when Sue awoke. How exciting this was and still is! As we ended our prayer session that morning, I whispered to God, "Forgive me, Father, if this is my lack of faith. I have received visions about how a service might go in the past, but the service didn't happen that way. It would be nice to have confirmation of my dream."

On Sunday, Novebmer 1, Sue and I attended church; then, we enjoyed lunch with friends at a local restaurant. Having eaten, we were saying our goodbyes in the parking lot. Deborah, who told my wife after our wedding that we would be moving back, walked up and said, "Ferel, God just released me to tell you that I had a vision and message last night. A man stood before me that was short and wearing a red shirt. You would meet this man in the Dominican Republic and heal him."

I could hardly contain myself as she was speaking. As soon as she finished, I told her that I had a dream with other information about this man. God had given me his name and his son's name also. We both shouted and had a moment of joy in Jesus by jumping up and down in the parking lot! WOW! AMAZING! GOD IS SO GOOD! This confirmation increased my faith immensely, removing all doubt!

My excitement grew, waiting for the trip to begin ten days later. I flew to Atlanta a day earlier to make flight connections easier on the day of departure. This would enable me to see dear friends who had relocated near Atlanta. They met me at the motel that evening for supper. I could hardly contain myself as I told them about the dream I had with my friend's confirmation. They listened graciously, but the look in their eyes told me that they were a little unsure about all I was relating. That didn't matter to me. I had become bold as a lion from all that had transpired previously. I knew in my heart that God wanted me to share what was happening; so, when it happened, their faith would be strengthened.

Arising by 5:00 am the next morning, I managed to take the first bus from the motel to the airport. I was glad I did! I had to enter one area of the airport and then take a tram to another terminal where all foreign flights departed. The invisible hand of God was always there to provide a timely person when I needed help. This provision that God prepared for me on every foreign mission trip is an astounding miracle!

As we met for our departure to the Dominican Republic, I discovered that there would be only five of us, one other couple including the group leader and wife. Though we were on the same plane, we were seated far apart, so getting acquainted was not conducive. We arrived in Santo Domingo midafternoon. We were picked up by the mission director and staff member in a 12-person van. Over 3 million people resided in this metro area. Driving to our accommodations, 10 miles away, took about two hours. It was quite an experience. Most of the time, we were riding in two or three-lane traffic, bumper-to-bumper, horns blaring, with bicycles weaving in and out between the cars. If my window had been opened, I could've touched them as they rode by. Sometimes traffic lights were not adhered to either, as drivers turned when they were not supposed to. We safely arrived at our destination. I breathed a sigh of relief. Our accommodations were nice, clean, and comfortable within a modern apartment complex. We spent the rest of the day getting acquainted and going over our itinerary for the week.

Prior to our first gathering at a local church the following day, I approached our team leader. I shared briefly about the dream and confirmation received concerning the pastor that I was to meet. I sought his advice on how to find him without disturbing the meetings and requested permission to minister to him either during or after the meeting. Thanking me for sharing with him, our team leader offered advice on how to proceed. He also informed me that I would be speaking at the afternoon gathering. The night service would be held there and also be attended by pastors and families in the area. The other two ladies of our team would speak that night. I thought to myself later that if this format followed, God would have to reveal to me if the pastor was present. I also hoped that two men would not be wearing a red shirt! Needless to say, I was anxious to meet the "man" in my vision.

Traffic was horrible as we returned to the church for the evening service. Traveling in the 5:00 pm traffic took an hour and a half on a trip that had taken only 30 minutes that morning. Looking out the window as we rode in the van, I quietly asked God, "How and when do I pray over this land? There's no way to have them pull over in this traffic."

I felt God say to my spirit, *"Just pray quietly in the van as you ride. Pray quietly over the land wherever you walk."*

"Yes, Lord, I can do that!" I replied.

A local pastor and his wife joined us on the second day and traveled with us throughout the week. Helping her set up a table for literature, I overheard her tell another volunteer that our mission director wanted every pastor and wife who attended to register. It suddenly dawned on me that registering would help solve my problem of finding the pastor that I was supposed to meet. She got excited as I briefly told her about the dream and my purpose in meeting him. She assured me that she would let me know if he attended the meeting by giving her his name.

The week was quickly passing. At every meeting, we witnessed many signs, wonders, and miracles occurring by the power of the Holy Spirit. I was disappointed that I still hadn't met the pastor in the red shirt. On November 19, our 2:00 pm session didn't begin until 3:15, as the people started to arrive around 3:00 pm. This church was very small and located within an impoverished area of Santo Domingo. A woman was the church's pastor. There were thirty-two in attendance. As I shared my message and demonstrated how to pray the verse, *"Enter his gates with thanksgiving, and his courts with praise! Give thanks to him; bless His name,"[3]* I was lifting thanksgiving and praise when His presence descended on me. I couldn't continue to speak. I was finally able to continue as my tears subsided. My message finished, I started to take my seat when the director's wife came up and stopped me. She said, "The Lord told me to have you close the service by praying corporately over everyone to receive this relationship into their hearts. Pray for God's spirit of intimacy to come alive within them."

The presence of the Lord came even stronger. I began to pray the prophetic declaration that I had received in October at my home. As this declaration came forth, the glory of the Lord filled this place! It felt passionate, powerful, and overwhelming! I knew by the Spirit that the "prophetic vein" had been RELEASED over the Dominican Republic. Our team and I were literally blown away! The people were standing, shouting, and clapping. God's glory subsided. The pastor closed the meeting.

Later as we were leaving, the team leader remarked, "Isn't this just like God to choose this small humble setting with fewer than 40 people. We had over 200 yesterday."

As he said that, I interjected, "Yes, I'm reminded how Jesus was born in a small, humble setting as well."

ASTONISHING! God's ways are not our ways! He chose to release His prophetic declaration in this small, modest, and out-of-the-way church.

During the team meeting Friday night, leadership instructed me that I would speak the next afternoon. They believed (as I did) that the Holy Spirit would manifest again to release the 'prophetic vein' declaration. I was excited!   We were sad to see our final day of ministry arrive. So many blessings had been given and received. We journeyed three hours to San Francisco de Macoris arriving at the church a half-hour before the afternoon session. The trip from Santo Domingo reflected the beautiful countryside, with small mountains on our left and right. Closer to where we were going, it became flat land with rice farming as the major crop. We came to our destination, a clean and modern city of one million, appearing more prosperous than Santo Domingo.

As we waited outside for the church to open, my spirit jumped inside of me. I would finally meet the pastor in the red shirt and fulfill my other purpose in coming. Ten minutes before our meeting began, I checked with the lady who was registering the pastors and wives, but the name seen in my vision had not registered.

The church was almost full, with around two hundred in attendance. I confess that I felt discouraged. Then I recalled Deborah, who confirmed my dream by her vision. My faith and hope were renewed.

As I sat in front, waiting for the meeting to start, the Spirit led me to say to another team member, "I know how disappointed you must feel about not getting to speak today. I know, I would be. I feel that you're anointed to close this service with your healing proclamation. The Spirit will guide us both."

Her countenance brightened as she quietly began preparing. I wouldn't realize until later how important this word would be.

The presence of the Holy Spirit was heavy and undeniable. God had prepared me for this moment. How great a joy to encounter God's Spirit this way! There was a bluish hue inside the church. Its interior was also painted blue and white. Before I began to speak, praying silently in the Spirit, the director's wife joined me at the pulpit. She instructed the pastors to prepare to receive what the Holy Spirit would say through me because this was an important word for their nation and ministry. The Holy Spirit came quickly! The prophetic word again exploded with power, conviction, and passion! It was received with shouting, clapping, standing, and praising God as before. AN EXPLOSIVE ATMOSPHERE! Upon its completion, I turned to give the mission director the microphone. He said, "Start your testimony!"

My testimony was well-received; praise God! I could see agreement, transformation in their eyes, and hearts filled with passion for our Lord. It was truly a time of experiencing Paul's "unspeakable joy."

Caught up in the moment as I finished, I started to sit down, but the director's wife jumped up and said, "Don't forget to announce your man's name."

I thanked her. Turning back to the congregation, I quickly asked anyone to come forward that had this name and also announced his son's name. God had given me a vision for him, containing a personal message. No response. My heart sank. My spirit said, however, "He's here!"

I asked again—no response. Leaving the podium, my team member came forward, delivering a healing declaration and altar call.

I left for a break, lingering in the back of the building; I was excited yet wondering, *where is the man, Lord?*

Fifteen minutes later, while I was drinking tea and sitting alone, the director's wife unexpectedly walked up and excitedly said, "I believe your man is here!"

Tears came into my eyes. He was sitting on the back row not more than fifteen feet away, talking to our interpreter and the director's wife. As Deborah had stated in the parking lot, he was small in stature and wearing a red open-collared shirt. *How could I forget to look for the red shirt?* WOW! We agreed to talk after the service.

As the program continued, the interpreter came over to explain why the pastor hadn't stood up when he heard his name called. He explained that hearing the middle name of his son confused him. It was hard to interpret into Spanish where the father resided in the North Country; therefore, his son's first name was correct, but the middle name was pronounced differently. Very similar, but with a small variation. Thank God that His purpose would not be denied; he was here! God works in wondrous ways, His beauty to behold!

GOD'S PURPOSE WILL NOT BE DENIED. HE WORKS IN WONDROUS WAYS!

"'For my thought are not your thoughts, neither are your ways my ways,' declares the Lord. 'As the heavens are higher than the earth, so are my ways higher than your ways and my thoughts than your thoughts.'"[4]

The man in the red shirt and I were standing together after the service awaiting the interpreter. I was eager and ready to go. *Where was he?* Looking around, I saw him standing by a woman with the team member's wife who closed the service. Unknown to me, they were having a conversation with this pastor's wife. I heard in my spirit, "Be patient. You've been waiting for this moment, so it won't hurt you to wait a little longer."

I replied, "Sorry, Lord. Yes, it's your agenda, not mine!"

When they were finished, the pastor's wife and the interpreter joined us. The Lord's presence was heavy. It brought restoration and healing to both of them. The Holy Spirit directed my conversation first to him. One lesson I quickly learned was never to assume what is received by God. My dream had seen a pastor in severe grief and depression over the death of his son. I assumed a physical death, but the father explained his son was dead spiritually. He was twenty-two and had denied his religious upbringing. I listened, prayed, and counseled the grieving dad.

Then I delivered the message to him, "I've called you to be a shepherd of My sheep. I love you very much and have brought this servant from a foreign land as confirmation of My love for you. Stop your grieving! I know your heart and love for Me! Feed My sheep! If I can do this for you, don't you think I'm capable enough to handle your son? Give him to Me!"

Then his wife received prophetic words; then they received words together. The Lord wanted them to become equally yoked and be a team in ministry. Other conversations occurred between us. This divine appointment had ended. What I didn't know at the time was what the Lord had been doing with his wife before our conversation. Afterward, I would discover how God used this dream to impact and bless others in bringing His will and kingdom to earth in ways that I could never have imagined. It's a multiplication of blessings for others.

I sat down alone, overwhelmed by all that had just taken place. My dream about this pastor and son proved again to me, beyond a shadow of a doubt, HOW REAL GOD IS! OUR LORD IS ALIVE! The power of the Holy Spirit manifested, bringing about His kingdom on earth. His presence is alive today, just as it was in the first century. *"Jesus Christ is the same yesterday, and today, and forever."*[5]

God's unfailing love for this pastor, son, and family was so overwhelming! The realization that God brought me over 2,000 miles to restore this pastor just as He had taken me over 2,000 miles to Venezuela 35 years ago to restore me as a pastor. That's a STUNNING MIRACLE! It's mindboggling! Seeing how God orchestrates people, time, and events at a divine moment to bring about His will on earth and transform one life is exhilarating! After meeting with this pastor and wife, I would soon discover just how "strategic" this dream was for God's plan to be fully accomplished. We are to give what we receive.

The other team couple began to tell the rest of this encounter. They explained how the pastor's wife had grabbed the interpreter after the service telling them what had happened. She had been in severe pain for six months with cysts across her chest and breast. During the corporate prayer for healing, she felt her pain instantly cease. All the cysts were dissolved! She confessed her faith had been restored.

God's grand design is always bigger and better than anything we can imagine! God used another team member in her giftings. Another shared blessing is the principle of multiplication. This principle is similar to the young lad who gave Jesus two fish and five loaves that fed the five thousand. God works through willing and obedient followers who partner with Him in bringing His will and kingdom on earth. God fulfilled the deepest desire of my heart to serve Him again in a foreign land after thirty-five years. God's acts of abiding love become the substance and heart of **Hope Beyond.**

ENDNOTES

1. Psalm 40:8 ESV.
2. John 15:5.
3. Psalm 100:4 ESV.
4. Isaiah 55:8-9.
5. Hebrews 13:8.

ᴛHE MOSES MANDATE

God orchestrated time, people, and events for Moses' survival. At the age of eighty, Moses received a direct mandate from God; *"So now, go. I am sending you to Pharaoh to bring my people, the Israelites, out of Egypt."*[1]

My biblical understanding of the mandate is based on Moses receiving God's call or assignment to free His Hebrew people from the Egyptians. When completed, this specific directive from God to Moses would be finished. I believe that specific mandates from God can come during any season of life and that they are for God's purposes in bringing His kingdom to earth.

This experience Moses had at the age of eighty deepened my resolve that ministry with purpose was possible as I approached my eightieth birthday. When people asked me what was happening spiritually in my life prior to my eightieth birthday, I would often remark that I was preparing to receive my "Moses Mandate." Sometimes I might see a smirk or a smile creep across their face. Sometimes, as I said those words, I felt inwardly foolish. I truly believed, however, if God could use Moses at eighty, why not me?

Then I would think again of Moses. After receiving God's mandate to free the Hebrew people from Egypt, Moses immediately began to argue with God about how unworthy he was to do any task for Him. Reading this, I felt better about my reactions. Feeling unworthy seemed to be a normal reaction from many who stood in God's presence. What I learned from Moses' experience, however, was that God would provide whatever was needed for the task to be completed. As Paul wrote, *"But he said to me, 'My grace is sufficient for you, for my power is made perfect in weakness. Therefore, I will boast all the more gladly about my weaknesses, so that Christ's power may rest on me.'"*[2]

Whether working for a corporation, being pastor of a church, or owning my own business, my personality has basically been the same. I would receive a thought and create a strategic plan for accomplishing what had to be done. Whenever that task was completed, I was ready to begin again.

I have concluded that my life's journey can be divided into three distinct seasons of 27 years each. Chapter sixteen detailed the previous two seasons ending in June 1994. The third ended in June 2021. The last years of the third season have been spent committed to cultivating a more intimate, personal relationship with Jesus, my Lord. The heavenly Father honored my commitment in drawing closer to Him;

"Draw near to God, and he will draw near to you."[3]

During this process, God expanded my spiritual understanding and maturity through revelation by connecting and aligning strategic events. My eightieth year was a transitional year similar to transitional events that happened at the end of each previous season. What a blessing! What a journey! The best is yet to come!

There is a deep desire within me to finish my race strong in this final, fourth season! This brings me to the present time. I'm able to say with confidence and assurance that God knows my name, and I know Him! God loves me, and I love Him.

Even as I write this book, my heavenly Father continues to reveal truth. It's an ongoing process. God speaks through the prophet Jeremiah, saying, *"Call to me and I will answer you and tell you great and unsearchable things you do not know."*[4]

A deep yearning arose within me to share my experiences. Like a doubting Thomas, I had to be shown the reality of the living God and His risen Son, Jesus Christ. And the Lord answered me, and said; *"Write the vision and engrave it plainly on [clay] tablets so that the one who reads it will run. For the vision is yet for the appointed [future] time it hurries toward the goal [of fulfillment]; it will not fail. Even though it delays, wait [patiently] for it, because it will certainly come; it will not delay."*[5] By traveling this spiritual journey with me, you have read what I have experienced. My mandate in relating this journey has been to persuade the believer in Christ to grow in intimacy with Him. It's been to open the heart, mind, and soul of the unbeliever so they can discover His amazing love. Believe me, a person must live life with Jesus to comprehend it! If, through God's grace and power, the purposes in writing this book are fulfilled, my first "Moses Mandate" will be accomplished.

It's been astounding how methodical God has been in my spiritual journey. Without God's incredible love pouring forth through Jesus and His Holy Spirit, there would have been no divine appointments with the six obedient and bold women and my deliverance friend. They corrected my journey at just the right moment. Their prophetic messages from God redirected the pathway that He desired me to travel. There would not have been two lovely women that God sent to calmly share in the many ups and downs of my journey.

Nita, my companion for more than 50 years, stood alongside me during both seasons of ministry. Our 27 years in the wilderness became a process of redemption and restoration. Similar to the butterfly who struggles in the cocoon to be free, God's grace and our perseverance enabled us to endure and learn from our struggles and pain that often opens the gateway for wisdom, light, and transformation. This process prepared us for returning to the pastorate.

"Friends, when life gets really difficult, don't jump to the conclusion that God isn't on the job. Instead, be glad that you are in the very thick of what Christ experienced. This is a spiritual refining process, with glory just around the corner."[6]

Through it all, Nita was an encourager, always smiling, always joking, a friend to all until her death.

Being drawn to a similar personality, Sue entered my life. Sue, like Nita, is outgoing, loving, an encourager, and a friend to all, but different by possessing an independent spirit and extravagant generosity. Her favorite phrase is "You can't outgive God," though she tries. Her spiritual insight and wisdom gleaned from life's challenges, praying over the land, and her intercession at the International House of Prayer complements my spiritual journey. Sue's exposure to the prayer-prophetic movement, prophetic friends, and our daily prayers together cultivates an atmosphere and hunger for greater intimacy with Jesus. Intimacy is an ongoing process as we run with God's goodness, love, and grace.

I thank God for these two wonderful companions; Nita in active ministry to the church and Sue in furthering my spiritual growth and intimacy with Jesus.

What lies ahead? No one can really perceive the future, can they? Therefore, let us be thoroughly equipped and prepared for whatever season we may encounter.

Together, Sue and I are determined to enter our final season committed to "... *run with endurance the race that is set before us, looking to Jesus, the founder and perfecter of our faith ...*"[7] because "... *we are His workmanship, created in Christ Jesus for good works, which God prepared beforehand, that we should walk in them.*"[8]

During recent prayer times, I continue hearing two words: "**persevere**" and "**clarion**!" For me, persevere means to push ahead and never give up regardless of the circumstance!

> *"Therefore, put on the full armor of God, so that when the day of evil comes, you may be able to stand your ground, and after you have done everything ... STAND!"*[9]

Researching the word clarion, I discovered that it was associated with a medieval trumpet that emits a loud and unique tone. It was often blown as a call to action. I believe that God continues a "clarion call to action," corporately to the church, the Body of Christ, and personally to His faithful and obedient followers. Together, we answer God's brilliantly clear call to partner with Him in bringing His kingdom to earth. Our response to God's call becomes our legacy. His story is our present, becomes our past, and will be our future.

I believe that the most complete and fulfilling life is to discover God's unending love. By responding with perseverance to God's clarion call, we are made complete in Him.

"Brothers, I do not consider myself yet to have taken hold of it. But one thing I do: Forgetting what is behind and straining toward what is ahead, I PRESS ON ..."[10]

The sound of God's trumpet will draw us ever onward and upward until we breathe our last breath. In the twinkling of an eye, all who believe will join our Lord by sharing in His promise of resurrection. He becomes our final destination and ultimate **Hope Beyond** as we return home to the One who created us.

This book is God's story that became my story, and **Hope Beyond** can become your story as well. If you haven't already, try God; you might like Him!

"What, then, shall we say in response to these things?"[11]

HOPE BEYOND!

"WE HAVE THIS HOPE AS AN ANCHOR FOR THE SOUL, FIRM AND SECURE. IT ENTERS THE INNER SANCTUARY BEHIND THE CURTAIN, WHERE JESUS, WHO WENT BEFORE US, HAS ENTERED ON OUR BEHALF."[12]

ENDNOTES

1. Exodus 3:10.
2. 2 Corinthians 12:9.
3. James 4:8a ESV.
4. Jeremiah 33:3.
5. Habakkuk 2:2-3 AMP.
6. 1 Peter 4:12-13 MSG.
7. Hebrews 12:1-2 ESV.
8. Ephesians 2:10 ESV.
9. Ephesians 6:13.
10. Philippians 3:13-14a.
11. Romans 8:31a (See Romans 8:31-39 for the complete passage.)
12. Hebrews 6:19-20a.

THE MOST COMPLETE AND FULFILLING
LIFE POSSIBLE COMES WHEN WE
DISCOVER GOD'S UNENDING LOVE.

ͲHE ϹHOICE:
WHAT DO YOU SAY IN RESPONSE?

God delights in doing extraordinary things through ordinary people. You have a decision before you. Do you want to discover the God who orchestrates time, people, and events so that you can live life to the fullest and partner with Him in bringing about His will on earth?

Have you ever felt like something is amiss? Have you said these words? "I'm not satisfied with my life. I yearn for something more that offers purpose and fulfillment. I seek 'truth' that I can believe in and which will sustain me."

Finding what you seek begins with the fear of God.

"The fear of God is the beginning of wisdom ..."
—PSALM 111:10A

The *"fear of God"* is to worship, glorify, esteem, honor, respect, and adore Him.[1]

Are you ready to acknowledge God's incredible call to receive Him and begin to know more of Him? If you are, then **this holy fear of God is the starting point—an invitation to seek out His mysteries—the great unsearchable things your spirit cries out to comprehend.**

"Call to me and I will answer you and tell you great and unsearchable things you do not know."

—JEREMIAH 33:3

God's invitation is an ancient decision that every person must make.

"Multitudes, multitudes, in the valley of decision! For the day of the Lord is near in the valley of decision.

—JOEL 3:14 ESV

"Now fear the Lord and serve him with all faithfulness. Throw away the gods your ancestors worshiped beyond the Euphrates River and in Egypt, and serve the Lord. But if serving the Lord seems undesirable to you, then choose for yourselves this day whom you will serve, whether the gods your ancestors served beyond the Euphrates, or the gods of the Amorites, in whose land you are living. But as for me and my household, we will serve the Lord."

—JOSHUA 24:14 –15

Can it be that you are subconsciously seeking to return to the God who created you?

"The Lord God formed the man from the dust of the ground and breathed into his nostrils the breath of life, and the man became a living being."
—GENESIS 2:7

"The heroes all died still clinging to their faith, not even receiving all that had been promised them. But they saw beyond the horizon fulfillment of their promises and gladly embraced it from afar. They all lived their lives on earth as those who belonged to another realm. For clearly, those who live this way are longing for the appearing of a heavenly city. And if their hearts were still remembering what they left behind, they would have found an opportunity to go back. But they couldn't turn back for their hearts were fixed on what was far greater, that is the heavenly realm! So, because of this God is not ashamed in any way to be called their God, for he has prepared a heavenly city for them."
—HEBREWS 11:13-16 TPT

God the Father is calling to you. He formed you while you were in your mother's womb, and He has continuously orchestrated people and events to bring you to the place where you will recognize His voice and be ready to be reconciled back to Him through His Son, Jesus.

Jesus prays for you.

"And I ask not only for these disciples, but also for all those who will one day believe in me through their message. I pray for them all to be joined together as one even as you and I, Father, are joined together as one. I pray for them to become one with us so that the world will recognize that you sent me.

"For the very glory you have given to me I have given them so that they will be joined together as one and experience the same unity that we enjoy. You live fully in me and now I live fully in them so that they will experience perfect unity, and the world will be convinced that you have sent me, for they will see that you love each one of them with the same passionate love that you have for me.

"Father, I ask that you allow everyone that you have given to me to be with me where I am! Then they will see my full glory—the very splendor you have placed upon me because you have loved me even before the beginning of time. You are my righteous father, but the unbelieving world has never known you in the perfect way that I know you! And all those who believe in me also know that you have sent me! I have revealed to them who you are and I will continue to make you even more real to them, so that they may experience the same endless love that you have for me, for your love would now live in them, even as I live in them!"

—JOHN 17:20–26 TPT

Did you know that Jesus prays for you? That's pretty incredible when you think about it. Jesus wants to see you restored back to the Father, as clean as newly fallen snow, your sins completely wiped clean, so you can stand before God with confidence and receive His grace. That's why He prays for you. **Jesus wants God to become real to you. All you need to do is accept this priceless gift of reconciliation.** Would you like to know how to do that?

Simply ask Jesus to come into your heart. Say this prayer out loud to your heavenly Father and to His Son Jesus:

Jesus, come into my heart.

Forgive me of all my sin.

I believe by faith, Jesus, that You become my Savior, Lord, and friend.

Thank you, Jesus, for Your love, Your forgiveness, and Your gift of eternal life through the resurrection; in Jesus' name I pray, amen.

Bible Verses About Salvation

Here are a few verses from scripture that talk about God's gift of salvation for you:

> *"For God so loved the world that he gave his one and only son, that whoever believes in him shall not perish but have eternal life."*
>
> —JOHN 3:16

> *"For by grace you have been saved through faith. And this is not your own doing; it is the gift of God, not a result of works, so that no one may boast."*
>
> —EPHESIANS 2:8–9 ESV

> *"Because, if you confess with your mouth that Jesus is Lord and believe in your heart that God raised him from the dead, you will be saved."*
>
> —ROMANS 10:9 ESV

> *"Therefore, if anyone is in Christ, he is a new creation. The old has passed away; behold, the new has come."*
>
> —2 CORINTHIANS 5:17 ESV

WHAT'S NEXT?

Now that you have accepted Christ as your Savior, you want to get to know Him more. One great way to do that is to read the Holy Bible. As you study it, you'll discover all that you have been seeking through God's promises. I suggest beginning with John's Gospel, then Matthew, Mark, and Luke. These are the stories of Jesus while He was living on earth. Once you have read the Gospels, I suggest you read about the early Church in the book of Acts. After that, Romans and Psalms. Psalms reflect the emotions common to everyone.

Here are additional scriptures to encourage you on this new adventure:

"...There's nothing like the written Word of God for showing you the way to salvation through faith in Christ Jesus. Every part of Scripture is God-breathed and useful one way or another—showing us the truth, exposing our rebellion, correcting our mistakes, training us to live God's way. Through the Word, we are put together and shape for the tasks God has for us."
—2 TIMOTHY 3:14-17 MSG

"You make known to me the path of life; you will fill me with joy in your presence, with eternal pleasures at your right hand."
—PSALM 16:11

"'For I know the plans I have for you,' declares the Lord, 'plans to prosper you and not to harm you, plans to give you a hope and future.'"
—JEREMIAH 29:11

"And you are in Him, made full and have come to fullness of life—in Christ you too are filled with the God-head: Father, Son, and Holy Spirit, and reach full spiritual stature."

—COLOSSIANS 2:10a AMP

HOPE BEYOND!

"WE HAVE THIS HOPE AS AN ANCHOR FOR THE SOUL, FIRM AND SECURE. IT ENTERS THE INNER SANCTUARY BEHIND THE CURTAIN, WHERE JESUS, WHO WENT BEFORE US, HAS ENTERED ON OUR BEHALF."

HEBREWS 6:19-20A

ENDNOTE

1. *Bible in One Year 2021* with Nicky and Pippa Gumbel. Day 267 of the Devotional.

WHAT IS A PROPHETIC MESSENGER?

A PROPHETIC MESSENGER IS BIBLICAL

"For the testimony of Jesus is the spirit of prophecy."

REVELATION 19:10B

A PROPHETIC MESSENGER RECEIVES GOD'S GIFT

"Pursue love … desire the spiritual gifts, especially that you may prophesy … the one who prophesies speaks to people for their upbuilding and encouragement and consolation."

1 CORINTHIANS 14: 1, 3 ESV

A PROPHETIC MESSENGER IS THE RESULT OF GOD'S ETERNAL LOVE

"The Lord, the God of their Fathers, sent word to them again and again by His messengers, because He had compassion on His people and His dwelling place."

2 CHRONICLES 36:15 AMP

A PROPHETIC MESSENGER IS GOD'S MESSENGER

"For prophecy never had its origin in the will of man, but men spoke from God as they were carried along by the Holy Spirit."

2 PETER 1:21

"... what good will I be to you unless I bring you some revelation or knowledge or prophecy or word of instruction?"

1 CORINTHIANS 14:6

A PROPHETIC MESSENGER IS THE RECIPIENT

"Trust in the Lord with all your heart and lean not on your own understanding; in all your ways acknowledge Him and He will make your paths straight."

PROVERBS 3:5-6

A PROPHETIC MESSENGER CREATES AN EXPECTATION AND RESPONSIBILITY

- God orchestrates time, people, and events whenever He directs a believer, inspired by the Holy Spirit, to deliver His message to a specific person for His kingdom purpose. Paul differentiates this New Testament gift of prophecy from the office of an Old Testament prophet as he instructs the Corinthian church to judge each other's words.

> *"Let two or three prophets speak, and let the others weigh what is said."*
>
> 1 CORINTHIANS 14:29 ESV

- God's prophetic word received may be sought after or unexpected.

- The recipient of the word from God to be delivered has the responsibility to discern God's true intent and purpose in giving this word to the person at this specific time. This process requires that we spend time with the Lord in prayer and reading God's Word.

> *"Don't suppress the Spirit, and don't stifle those who have a word from the Master. On the other hand, don't be gullible. Check out everything, and keep only what's good. Throw out anything tainted with evil."*
>
> 1 THESSALONIANS 5:19-22 MSG

God orchestrates time, people, and events so that every person can live life to the fullest and partner with him in bringing about his will on earth.

If you would like to invite Ferel Little to minister to your group or congregation, please connect with him at

WWW.FERELLITTLE.COM

Made in the USA
Middletown, DE
16 January 2022